695

1

Manuel Machado

MANUEL MACHADO

A REVALUATION

❦

GORDON BROTHERSTON

Lecturer in the Department of Literature,
University of Essex

CAMBRIDGE

AT THE UNIVERSITY PRESS

1968

Published by the Syndics of the Cambridge University Press
Bentley House, 200 Euston Road, London, N.W. 1
American Branch: 32 East 57th Street, New York, N.Y. 10022

Library of Congress Catalogue Card Number: 68–11281
Standard Book Number: 521 04334 4

Printed in Great Britain
at the University Printing House, Cambridge
(Brooke Crutchley, University Printer)

CONTENTS

ILLUSTRATIONS

ACKNOWLEDGEMENTS

I should like to thank the following people for helping me with this book, and with the doctoral dissertation, submitted to the University of Cambridge in 1965, out of which it grew, considerably transformed: Fernán Alonso, Professor J. M. Blecua, Professor R. F. Brown, Sr. Campuzano, Sr. Casero, Hermana Eulalia (Machado's widow), Sr. García Morales, Sr. García Rámila, Mrs. H. F. Grant, Sr. Gullón, Robert Johnson, Gordon Minter, Sr. Nadal, Patricia O'Riordan, Dr A. K. G. Paterson, Sr. Penzol, Professor G. W. Ribbans, Sr. Ruiz Cabriada, Professor J. Tzerbrikov, Professor E. M. Wilson.

I am also indebted to the Ministry of Education for a State Studentship from 1961 to 1964, the period during which most of the documentary material for this book was collected, and to the staff of the following institutions for their ready help: the University Library and the Modern Languages Library at Cambridge; The Instituto de España, the Hispanic Council, the British Museum and the Colindale Newspaper Library in London; the Bibliothèque de l'Arsenal in Paris; the Biblioteca Nacional, the Hemeroteca Municipal and the Ministerio de Educación Nacional in Madrid; the Biblioteca de la Universidad (the old library) in Seville, the Archivo Miguel de Unamuno in Salamanca and the Biblioteca Machado in Burgos.

NOTES AND ABBREVIATIONS USED

Works both by and on Manuel Machado which are referred to by an abbreviated title in the book are described fully in the bibliography. Machado's poems are, however, listed under their titles in a separate index which gives details of published sources and important variants. Throughout, the Biblioteca Machado, Burgos, is referred to as the *BMB*.

The accentuation of Spanish words has been modernized where appropriate, and the following words have been Anglicized when they appear in an English sentence:

Andalucía	Andalusia
Coruña	Corunna
Modernismo, Modernista	Modernism, Modernist
Sevilla	Seville

INTRODUCTION

Manuel Machado's reputation, now so low, was once great and enviable. In the first quarter of this century he was known both in and outside the Spanish-speaking world as one of the three or four poets of his time in Spain. He was considered an important member of that literary renaissance which began more or less with Spain's defeat by the U.S.A. in 1898 and which terminated with the Civil War.

Machado began his career with the advantage of being intelligent and the son of one of the most cultured and informed intellectuals of late nineteenth-century Spain: Antonio Machado y Álvarez. This, combined with a long immersion in the life of Paris at the turn of the century, gave him an experience and a poise which distinguished him among his contemporaries, the Modernists, as they readily recognized. He was valued for his poetry, his conversation, his wit. His flat in Madrid was a meeting place for the Modernists and the cradle of the periodicals they planned and launched. And this pre-eminence he maintained, despite some turbid complications in his Bohemian and then his married life. By the 1920s his prestige was obvious, from the frequency and the tone of the references made to him as a public figure in reviews and magazines of that time, and from the fact that Antonio Machado was then thought interesting because he was the brother of Manuel.

Of all this, little remains or is remembered. Today, he is rarely considered even as a humble term of comparison with the consecrated names of Antonio Machado and Juan Ramón Jiménez. His escape from recognition is due partly to the original quality of that recognition: his was a personal fame, relying, like Gómez Carrillo's, on human presence and fashionable impact. It was all right as long as he was there to enliven the mass of journalism and occasional verse his position urged from him. Once he vanished, this mass became inert, and buried the few poems on which an enduring reputation might have rested.

But in Machado's case, sensitivity to present circumstance brought more than the usual perils of ephemerality. His malleability in 1936, then his immediate salvation, was ultimately the cause of a more ignominious ruin. The literary support he lent to General Franco's crusade removed him abruptly from the consideration of its opponents, among whom were counted most of the Spanish intellectuals.[1] To have extolled reaction was a base betrayal of more consequence than anything laudable he might have done before that date. And even within Nationalist Spain he did not fare much better in the end. His very enthusiasm, in its single-mindedness, became embarrassing once the killing was over and complexity and discrimination regained some sort of place in normal life. He lost, then, a claim to estimation in the eyes of both Spains.

There can be no doubt that his end was lamentable. But this has nothing to do with whether his earlier poetry is interesting or not, with whether books like *Alma* (1902), *Alma. Museo. Los Cantares* (1907), *El Mal Poema* (1909) and *Ars moriendi* (1921) do or do not contain good poems. This seems obvious. But since the Civil War few critics have in fact followed the indications of Machado's contemporary reviewers: Miguel de Unamuno, Enrique Díez-Canedo, Eduardo Gómez de Baquero, Jorge Guillén, Juan Chabás and others. Few have gone back to explore and reappraise, except perhaps for Dámaso Alonso in an incisive essay 'Ligereza y gravedad en la poesía de Manuel Machado'. More often his work has been treated as a scavenging ground by tired journalists and bureaucrats with literary pretensions. And his worst poems have for that reason had the most publicity.

This absence of critical rigour has fostered a tendency to easy characterization: Machado, the typical Sevillian who would sooner have been a bullfighter than a poet; the feeble-minded aristocrat who opted out of the struggle for life; the aesthete disdainful of common humanity. Some evidence may perhaps be found to support these descriptions; but stated thus baldly they are a parody of Machado's actual career in the labyrinthine society

[1] José Moreno Villa, however, grappled fruitfully with Machado's infidelity in his essay 'La Manolería y el cambio'.

he knew and lived in.[1] He did after all want with some passion to be a poet; his success was not the gift of laziness and a private income but of persistent effort; and he did involve himself purposefully in socialist movements of his time, especially after the first world war.

But in any case, this sort of approach, this urge to typify, encourages superficial or partial reading; it does not help towards a proper appreciation of what is important in Machado, or in any poet: poetry, poetic achievement. This would not matter if none of the poems which originally earned Machado his high reputation could stand scrutiny. As it is, some of them can, and ought to stand it. For, closely read, 'Felipe IV' proves Machado to be one of the most subtly concise poets writing in Spain before the first world war, 'La pena', the most sensitively Andalusian, and 'Eleusis', one of the most profound.

---

[1] Miguel Pérez Ferrero's *Vida de Antonio Machado y Manuel* is useful; but like Machado's own autobiographical *Unos versos, un alma y una época*, it is excessively vague and anecdotal. Despite its brevity, Pedro de Répide's article 'Lira y guitarra' is by contrast very informative. Much of the new material in this study is taken from the archives in the Biblioteca Machado, Burgos, and from José Machado's unpublished work *Últimas soledades del poeta Antonio Machado*.

1

SEVILLE, MADRID, SEVILLE
(1874–1897)

...yo mismo andaluz, sevillano
hasta la médula (de allí soy, de allí
mis padres y mis abuelos)
—Prologue to *Cante hondo*

What Manuel Machado said about his Andalusian origins in 'Adelfos', in the prologue to *Cante hondo* and certain late autobiographical works, suggests that he was a man with a background which was at once aristocratic, exotic and Spanish Catholic, a man whose early existence had evolved to the rhythm of a southern city where refined Moor, sensual gypsy and Holy Week penitent were one.[1] This suggestion, which has often been repeated by critics, has little biographical foundation. This is not to say that Machado's origins were not literally Andalusian. He was born in Seville, on 29 August 1874, and spent his childhood there; both his parents' families were Andalusian. But for the most part his self-characterization is misleading.

He was not an aristocrat. His mother, Ana Ruiz, was the daughter of a sweet-seller in Triana; his father, Antonio Machado y Álvarez, a middle-class intellectual, devoted much of his life to undermining the social system which conferred on him such superiority as he had. Machado y Álvarez had supported the revolution of 1868, in which his father, Antonio Machado y Núñez, had played an important role as a member of the radical Revolutionary junta in Seville and later as governor of the province.[2] Machado y Álvarez was even more radical, and certainly less circumspect, than his father. With the return of the Bourbons

[1] See *Unos versos*, pp. 20–5, and the autobiographical parts of *Estampas sevillanas*.
[2] Details of his difficulties as governor survive in the *BMB* in his correspondence with Rivero, Moret, Sagasta and others. C. A. M. Hennessy mentions his case in Chapter 3 of *The Federal Republic in Spain* (Oxford, 1962).

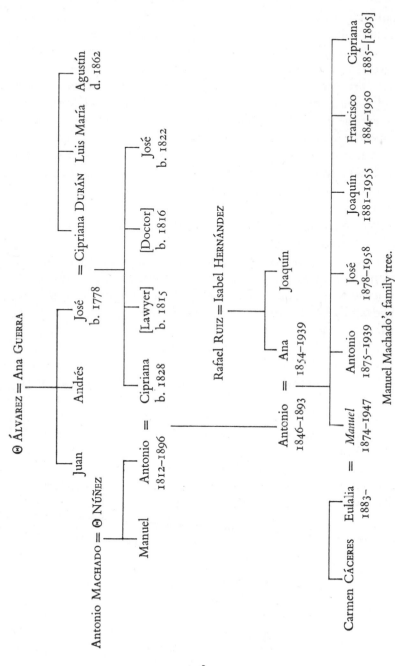

Manuel Machado's family tree.

and the proclamation of Alfonso XII as king in 1874, an event which coincided with his marriage and the birth of his first son Manuel, Machado y Álvarez lost his job as a lawyer and devoted himself to disturbing the calm of his household and his country with protests against the immorality of the civil administration and against social injustice.[1] Nobody took any notice of him, except the group of Sevillian writers and academics in eclipse of which he was a member.[2] He thought to find an outlet for his frustrated idealism in Madrid, where he moved in 1883 with his wife, who was now expecting their fifth child, joining the general exodus from the provinces to the capital in late nineteenth-century Spain. Following Sagasta's liberal reinterpretation of the constitution of the Universidad Central of Madrid and Giner de los Ríos's reinstatement there in 1881, Machado y Núñez, a friend of Giner's and a biologist by profession, was appointed Dean of the Faculty of Sciences; it was this appointment that caused the Machados to uproot themselves permanently from Andalusia. The family lived together in one flat, for Machado y Álvarez had still not found a job. Indeed, he never found one. The history of this latter part of his brief life is one of a hopeless struggle to establish democratic liberalism, to foster an enlightened attitude towards the sciences and to support himself, the father of six children, in the Spain of the *Restauración*. The little influence and success he had, he had abroad not at home. As an anthropologist and the founder in 1881 of the first folk-lore society in Spain, he was asked by the Philological Society to read papers in London; but in Madrid Sagasta, although an old family acquaintance, ignored his pleas for material help for projects like the *Biblioteca de tradiciones populares españolas*, a series of publications to which

[1] The main collections of articles and propaganda are: *Artículos religiosos y morales* (Madrid, 1883), *Batallas del Libre Pensamiento* (Madrid, 1885)—both under the pseudonym 'Demófilo'—and *Obras completas* (Madrid, 1904). His early collections of folk-lore material also have a strong political bias.

[2] See J. Guichot, *Historia de la ciudad de Sevilla* (Seville, 1886), L. Montoto, *Por aquellas calendas* (Madrid, 1930), and my article 'Machado y Álvarez and Positivism'; see also A. Sendras, 'Antonio Machado y Álvarez', *Revista de España*, CXLI (1892), pp. 279–91, J. Sama, 'Don Antonio Machado y Álvarez', *Boletín de la Institución libre de enseñanza*, 389 (30 June 1893), pp. 125–8 and A. Guichot, *Noticia histórica del folklore* (Seville, 1922).

he had already sacrificed the money he had. As the family moved from flat to flat downhill into dinginess he worked harder as a translator and a journalist, ever knocking at those ministerial doors Galdós has described so well. He died finally of a stroke and overwork in 1893, at the age of 46, after sailing alone to Puerto Rico to take up a minor Civil Service post that was eventually offered to him. The level of poverty to which the family sank is recorded by Manuel and Antonio Machado in articles they wrote in *La Caricatura*, at the time of their father's death, about the shabby area of Madrid they inhabited.[1] For the most part however, Manuel at least was silent about the unexotic indigence of his early life, and seldom referred to his father. Indeed, even when describing him as 'una de las más altas mentalidades de la pasada centuria',[2] he said nothing about what was at once Machado y Álvarez's main preoccupation and obstacle to fortune: his anticlericalism.

Manuel Machado's background was certainly not Spanish Catholic. From early childhood he was constantly exposed to demonstrations of the corruption of the church.[3] He repeatedly heard his father vituperate, for example, the Holy Week penitents, and the brotherhood of La Aurora, suppressed under the Republic and restored under the *Restauración*, whose practice it was to rouse the faithful to prayer by ringing handbells through the streets at dawn. Readers of the many articles Machado y Álvarez wrote against the church were excommunicated by the Synod of Seville and the bishop of Jaén; attempts were made to suppress the reviews and newspapers which published them. Such extremes of ill-will were usual in the Seville of Manuel Machado's childhood, where the *Restauración* was widely conceived of as an official blanket of orthodoxy thrown on the fires of fierce hatred for the church which had flared up when Seville was an independent

---

[1] Articles by 'Tablante de Ricamonte', *La Caricatura*, 54, 61 and 62 (July–September 1893).

[2] 'Acotación preliminar' to Machado y Álvarez, *Cantes flamencos*, Austral, Buenos Aires, 1947.

[3] In fact, one of the most powerful articles in *Artículos religiosos y morales*, 'A mi hijo', takes the form of an emphatic response to Manuel's puerile questioning of rightness of his father's hatred for the church.

canton and freethinkers and the populace alike had fought the faithful with fists and stones. Much of this popular outburst proved to be ephemeral[1] and inarticulate. In Machado y Álvarez's case, however, anticlericalism was an enduring tenet of his inherited freemasonry. He never forsook traditional masonic attitudes and supported his attacks with contemporary philosophical arguments, from the time he was a student and a Krausist,[2] to the late 'seventies and early 'eighties when his propagandistic energies redoubled under the stimulus of the Positivist and Evolutionary ideas which were then beginning to infiltrate into Spain.

Machado y Álvarez shared his anticlerical bias and his ideological development from Krausism to Positivism with other Sevillian intellectuals of the liberal university group, and more importantly with the founders of the *Institución libre de enseñanza*, where Manuel and his younger brothers began to go to school as soon as the family arrived in Madrid. The Machados were closely linked to the *Institución*. In the year of its foundation both Machado y Núñez and Machado y Álvarez had given books to the new library and Machado y Álvarez had dedicated his first folklore publications to the school as 'su más sincero admirador y amigo'. They knew Linares, Flores and M. B. Cossío; Joaquín Costa (who had close connections with the Sevillian group) and Sama were old friends, and Giner de los Ríos was intimate with them both. Giner was engaged to Machado y Álvarez's cousin María; the two men had known each other well when Machado y Álvarez was studying in Madrid before the 1868 rising and had often spent the night in discussion at Machado's lodgings. The high regard that the *Institucionistas* had generally for Machado y Álvarez is shown by the fact that they offered him a specially

---

[1] Even as late as 1882, however, a procession commemorating the bi-centenary of Murillo's death was enough to provoke a morning of savage street fighting (Guichot, *Historia de la ciudad de Sevilla*, p. 281).

[2] Krausism in Spain has had a complicated history. The movement, which was inspired initially by Sanz del Río (1814–69), a disciple of the German philosopher Krause (1781–1832), is better understood in terms of moral attitudes than as a philosophical doctrine. Further details can be found in the articles quoted in this chapter which deal with Machado y Álvarez and with the *Institución libre de enseñanza*.

created chair of folk-lore studies at the *Institución* in 1885, two years after he returned to Madrid with his family.[1]

Manuel Machado and his brothers Antonio and José began to attend the *Institución* when it was still in Calle Infantas and fights with a neighbouring Jesuit college were frequent. But the few memories Manuel published of his days at the school are of the larger grounds and lighter classrooms of its later home in the Paseo del Obelisco. The influence of the *Institución* on Manuel has generally been considered by critics as antithetical to, and less important than, that of Seville. This for example was the opinion of Federico de Onís: 'Sería difícil determinar la huella que la Institución dejase en su espíritu; sin duda no le prestó ninguno de los rasgos formales que distinguen a los institucionistas. En cambio es imborrable y esencial lo que en él quedó del ambiente sevillano.'[2] This is just, but with two qualifications. First: it is not true that Manuel Machado was not in sympathy, at least at the time of his education, with the ideals of Giner. His first poems not only reflect details of the visits, for which the *Institución* was noted, to the workshops, factories and smithies of Madrid, but also capture the feeling those visits were intended to provoke:

> También el hombre despertó. Ya suena
> el vigoroso golpe del martillo
> en el noble taller. Ya en las ciudades
> el continuo afanar...
> ....
> Aquí la ansiosa llama
> ruge en el horno, y en el fuerte hierro
> con su horrible calor vida derrama.
> ....

[1] J. Uña asked Machado to accept the chair in recognition of his work as a folk-lorist, 'y comprendiendo la transcendencia de los estudios folklóricos para el de nuestra historia y para el progreso y mejoramiento de nuestra cultura' (letter, Madrid, 27 September 1885, *BMB*). Sendras, *Revista de España*, CXLI (1882) refers to this appointment as 'un cargo que no llegó a desempeñar' without saying why. See also A. Jiménez-Landi, 'Don Francisco Giner de los Ríos y *La Institución libre de enseñanza*', *Revista Hispánica Moderna*, XXV (1959), 1–2, p. 38).

[2] *Antología de la poesía española*, p. 244; the Jesuit M. Linares, saw the *Institución* as a pernicious but mercifully not all-powerful influence: 'La fe, recibida en el bautismo, agostada, entre los racionalismos heterodoxos de la Institución... pero no muerta...' ('Manuel Machado habla de su espíritu'.)

¡Oh trabajo, oh labor! En vuestro seno
la humanidad entera se engrandece.　　　　　('Al día')

Before leaving the *Institución* at 15, to take his examinations at
Cardenal Cisneros, he acquired what he could not easily have
acquired at other schools of the time: a sense of the dignity of
work ('el noble taller') and great familiarity with European
history and culture, particularly from M. B. Cossío's art classes,
the effect of which is obvious in the poems of *Apolo*. His private
correspondence shows that he stayed as close as Antonio to Giner
and Cossío in later life. And whenever he passed the building in
the Paseo del Obelisco he thought of it as his alma mater and,
looking in at the large walled garden with its old walnut tree, he
would recall the days he spent there: 'Yo lo he corrido mil veces,
lo he cultivado, cavado, podado... ¡Oh días benditos!'[1] The
second qualification is of course that Manuel Machado's experience of the *Institución* was hardly antithetical to that of his native
city as the child of Machado y Álvarez. Indeed, if we are to understand Federico de Onís's distinction and relate meaningfully
Machado's formative environment with his claim to being
'sevillano hasta la médula', then we must turn not to his childhood
but to his late adolescence, to the period he spent in Seville away
from the rest of the family as an undergraduate.

Manuel Machado lived the greater part of the years 1895,
1896 and 1897 in Triana with his mother's parents, having been
sent to Seville to complete a much belated *bachillerato* and, by
special arrangement, to take concurrently a degree course in less
than the normal three years at the university, where his grand-
father was once rector.[2] During his absence in Madrid the atmosphere of Seville had changed and become indeed gayer and more
'southern' now that *Restauración* society was more confidently
established: that society of luxurious, newly-created aristocrats to
whom Manuel had the tact to dedicate many of the poems in his

[1] *La Guerra Literaria*, p. 101; for the importance of his education in *Apolo*, see
Chapter 11 below.
[2] Details of Machado's education are taken from the file under his name in the
archives of the Ministerio de Educación Nacional, Madrid; they often contradict
information given by other critics, M. Pérez Ferrero, J. Cejador y Frauca,
A. Moreno, and by Machado himself.

first verse collection *Tristes y Alegres*. The change of atmosphere was most evident in the university itself, once the stronghold of Republicans, Krausists and Positivists. By 1895 only two survivors of that time were left, Federico de Castro and Manuel Sales y Ferré, both University lecturers. Despite their old intimacy with the Machado family, Manuel nowhere mentions either of them, and Juan Ramón Jiménez, who unknown to Manuel was also a pupil of Castro's, spoke of Castro's pathetic isolation in that changed society.[1] Typical of this new group was Joaquín Hazañas, who taught two of the courses Manuel followed in his first year, Spanish literature (which he failed) and metaphysics. Hazañas, handsomely patronized by the Sevillian aristocracy, was a staunch monarchist. He was an equally staunch Roman Catholic and was well rewarded by the church for writing an ecclesiastical history of Seville which Machado y Álvarez would have found execrable. It was during this period that Manuel Machado first began to consider desirably and 'typically' Sevillian the elegant horse parades of the Feria, the Holy Week processions, the bullfights (abhorred by Giner) and the gypsy singers. He frequented the company of the gypsy *toreros* and *bandilleros* from La Cava and drank *manzanilla* with them in the *colmaos* 'La Marina' and 'La Laguna' He became a friend of his contemporary, Emilio Torres, the eldest of the three bullfighting brothers from Triana, and in Silverio Franconetti's famous café he became attuned to the cadences of *cante hondo*.

During this first of many long periods in Seville in late adolescence, when Antonio remained mostly in Madrid, Manuel Machado learnt the southern accent he used more or less discreetly later in life. His Seville was *Restauración* Seville, the 'Sevilla... torera y graciosa y animada' of his poems.[2] And this Seville was not the city he was born in, the brother of Antonio and the child of the unfortunate Machado y Álvarez.

[1] R. Gullón, *Conversaciones*, p. 57; when they saw that he respected Castro, Juan Ramón's companions asked him: 'Cómo tratas a ese krausista?'. Castro, a disciple of Sanz del Río's, once entrusted his chair at Seville to Machado y Álvarez during a temporary absence in 1871.

[2] *La fiesta nacional*, VI; he returned frequently to Seville to visit his cousin Eulalia Cáceres, to whom he became engaged in 1897; 'y ella una niña' ('Eulalia'). L. Doreste Silva, 'Los poetas se van'.

2

PARISIAN PERSPECTIVES

(1897–1902)

Cada hombre de espíritu tiene
dos patrias — la suya y París.
— *El Liberal*, 6 June 1918

The most important single event in Manuel Machado's life was his visit to Paris in 1899. As he himself recognized, the two years he spent in France as a young man in his mid twenties had a profound effect on his writing and his attitudes.

Before this experience his rôle and capacity as a writer were both minor. His very first poems, those published in *La Caricatura* and other literary journals, and in *Tristes y Alegres* (1895) and *Etcétera* (1896), joint collections with Enrique Paradas, are all firmly in the tradition of the bourgeois press of the 1890s. These poems were smart, world-weary quatrains, of the sort popularized by Campoamor and Núñez de Arce, expressing the thoughts of those moustached, cane-carrying gentlemen who were depicted in *La Caricatura* and who paraded the avenues of late nineteenth-century Madrid. Or they were exhortatory odes in the style and metre of Quintana, conforming to a convention of high-minded writing, for which, in Machado's particular case, Eduardo Benot was responsible. After the death of Machado y Álvarez and of Machado y Núñez, Benot, a writer of tedious and unimpeachable orthodoxy, acted as guardian to the Machado boys: they used to offer their compositions to his ready criticism at his formal *tertulia* at 6 Calle Villamagna on Sundays. Other poems in *Tristes y Alegres* smack of the gay vulgarity of the *género chico*, to which Manuel was introduced by his schoolfriends Ricardo Calvo and Joaquín Valverde (a fêted composer of *zarzuelas*) and by other members of the group which met at the café Fornos—'el bullicioso, alegre y escandaloso burdel de la juventud último tercio del pasado siglo'. Machado's witty gossip about the theatrical and bullfighting world and his always knowing the latest popular song or tango soon distinguished him in that company: another friend, Antonio de Zayas, remembered him as 'el decano de la asamblea literaria de Fornos'.[1] Even those 'angry' poems Machado wrote at this period, which purport to be a Bohemian protest against bourgeois values, were defiant in a fashion acceptable to that society. The gestures of 'Inmoral', for example, the first of Machado's self-portraits in verse, were thought no more offensive than the poems by Paradas which inspired them. Paradas, drunk in a bar with Miguel Sawa, may have cursed civilization as comprehensively as Espronceda, but this did not make him less welcome at Victoria Minelli's parties or prevent Benot from allowing him to edit a considerable number of issues of La Caricatura.[2]

Within the limits of this (stultifying) environment, Manuel Machado proved by the age of 21 or so that he was a fluent poet and even a competent writer of journalistic prose. He observed these limits, however, and avoided that stage of soul-searching and radical questioning through which, for example, Unamuno and Martínez Ruiz passed at a similar age. Much later in life he

[1] From a handwritten dedication to Machado of his translations from J.-M. de Hérédia, Los trofeos (Madrid, s.d.). Machado has a fine description of the evenings at Fornos, El amor, pp. 189–90. There are, besides, frequent references to this period and his association with Calvo and Zayas in his private letters and in the interesting dedication of Ars moriendi to Zayas: 'Hace 25 años que escribíamos juntos nuestros primeros versos.' He also recalled how they wrote poetry together at 'una tertulia en casa de Ricardo Calvo, formada por mi hermano Antonio, Calvo y Antonio de Zayas, hoy duque de Amalfi... Nuestra mayor afición era el teatro, teatro que escribíamos asimismo para ser representado por nosotros' (Rafael Narbona, 'El gran poeta Manuel Machado'). José Machado took a less than ideal view of his brothers' relationship with Calvo and Zayas, being irked by both Zayas's stupid snobbishness and Antonio's fitful dependence on Calvo's wealth (Últimas, p. 63).

[2] For Machado's remarks about Paradas, see La Guerra Literaria, p. 77 and Unos versos, p. 48. The Machados' contributions to La Caricatura were all made during the time of Paradas's editorship; Aurora de Albornoz, La prehistoria de Antonio Machado (Puerto Rico, 1961) has reproduced those by Antonio (but not those by Manuel) and has shown that Pérez Ferrero's account of the incident (Vida, p. 42) contains inaccuracies. Paradas's Esproncedan bravura is recorded by Miguel Sawa in his prologue to Paradas's first book Agonías (Madrid, 1891; omitted from J. M. de Cossío's otherwise thorough Cincuenta años); Manuel Machado himself wrote an epilogue to a second book, Undulaciones (Madrid, 1893).

13

claimed that, on the contrary, he had had his preoccupations. More than once he referred to the first performance of Joaquín Dicenta's *Juan José* in 1895 and to the innocent socialist and anti-clerical fervour it inspired in his generation. A 'reprise' in 1918 brought the following response:

> No quisiera rememorarlos aquellos días tan próximos ¡y tan pasados!, en que una 'élite' inteligente y fuerte, precursora de los renovadores puramente literarios y artísticos del 98, sentía ya acongojado su entusiasmo por algo así como el presentimiento de la gran catástrofe colonial y política y se debatía airada contra el 'statu quo' y el marasmo de su España de entonces. Se debatía y protestaba con motines, con asonadas, con libros subversivos y periódicos rojos. Vivía inquieta y desazonada. Vivió poco. Muchos acabaron jóvenes, víctimas de la bohemia a que los llevó su descontento y del alcohol en que ahogaron ansias de ideal. Sawa, Paso, Delorme. Otros cambiaron con los tiempos...[1]

But here we must beware of hindsight, which is the main support of Machado's double claim. First: although he says this élite preceded the '98 generation, in fact Sawa, Paso and Delorme were more active after 1895 than before. And the date '1898' itself is a guide and not an absolute term: had not Unamuno protested against the 'marasmo' of Spain already in 1895? Secondly: neither earlier nor later did Machado himself show any signs of being irritated by the 'status quo' in Spain. His signature is entirely absent from 'periódicos rojos' like *Germinal*, for which Delorme wrote articles on Marxism. The only evidence of his militancy in 'la guerra literaria' waged by the then indistinguishable *noventayochistas* and Modernists is two sonnets: one, 'Ella' published in Benavente's *Madrid Cómico* in December 1898 and the other, 'Lo que dicen las cosas', in *La vida literaria* in March 1899, just before his departure to Paris. These poems intimate a new sensibility and suggest that Machado had heard of Verlaine, probably through Alejandro Sawa (Miguel's elder brother), after Sawa's return from Paris in 1896.[2] But even so they violated no established precepts. Until he went to Paris himself, Machado hardly

---

[1] *Un año*, p. 57.
[2] 'Alejandro Sawa...bohemio incorregible, volvió por entonces de París hablando de parnasianismo y de simbolismo, y recitando por primera vez en Madrid versos de Verlaine. Pocos estaban en el secreto' (*La Guerra Literaria*, pp. 27–8). Sawa, who claimed he had closed Verlaine's eyelids before leaving Paris, was of course Máximo Estrella in Valle-Inclán's play *Luces de bohemia*.

transcended the provincial limits of his early literary environment:
and he showed striking awareness of this by later disowning all
he wrote before he left Spain for the first time.[1]

His decision to go to Paris was not that of a free spirit. He went
to get a job. In the eighteen months which separated his gradua-
tion from Seville University in September 1897 and his departure
from Spain in March 1899, the most sustained and profitable
employment he had found was helping Eduardo Benot from time
to time with the compilation of a *Diccionario de ideas afines*. With
Machado y Núñez's death in 1895 the economic position of the
Machado family had deteriorated; they lived together in a small,
barely furnished flat with brick floors in calle Fuencarral where the
low rent could be covered by the limited private income received
by Machado y Núñez's widow. To alleviate the situation one of
the younger grandsons—Joaquín—was dispatched to Guatemala
to earn his living as a farm hand, and Manuel went to Paris to
find jobs for himself and Antonio as translators in the Garnier
Frères publishing house.[2]

The two brothers lived and worked in the Latin Quarter when
Antonio joined Manuel in June. Their hotel, the Hôtel Medicis
where Verlaine had lived five years previously, was not far from
the Maison Garnier, which was, and still is, in the rue des Saints
Pères. They seem generally to have avoided their compatriots—

---

[1] His persistent desire to have *Alma* thought of as his 'primer libro de versos' is
confirmed by Juan Ramón Jiménez: 'Antonio Machado escribió un libro de
cantares, anterior a *Soledades* y Manuel, a sus 17 años [he was in fact 20],
publicó otro, que yo tenía y me lo robaron. Ellos procuraron destruir todos los
ejemplares y nunca más quisieron acordarse de tales libros' (R. Gullón, *Conversaciones*, p. 57). This, his subsequent disparagement of the age 'insulsa e
idiota' of the 'comediercos del género chico' (*La Guerra Literaria*, p. 23), and,
more important, the discontinuity between his youthful and his mature work
(see Chapters 8 and 9 below), all discourage the idea that Manuel Machado
suppressed his verse of the 'nineties only in order to be able to draw clandestinely
on it later. This, however, is the argument proposed by Orozco Díaz in 'Poesía
juvenil y juventud poética en la obra de Manuel Machado'.

[2] Joaquín Machado, 'Relámpagos'; José Machado, *Últimas*, pp. 25–6 and p. 60;
M. Pérez Ferrero, *Vida*, p. 49; R. Cansinos Assens, 'Juan Ramón Jiménez'.
Juan Ramón himself has the terse note: 'Madrid. Abuela queda viuda y regala
la casa. Madre inútil. Todos viven pequeña renta abuela. Casa desmantelada.
Familia empeña muebles. No trabajan, ya hombres. Casa de la picaresca. Venta
de libros viejos. Muere abuela' (*El Modernismo*, pp. 159–60).

political exiles, writers, singers, adventurers, card-sharpers and the like—who congregated in the bar Critérium opposite Saint Lazare station. They made an exception of Pío Baroja, whose stay in Paris coincided almost exactly with Antonio's; Baroja was embittered by failure to get a job even at Garnier's. They often ate together in a cheap restaurant frequented by workmen and the French Salvation Army. They became involved in the street fights provoked by the revision of the Dreyfus affair, and Baroja remembered Antonio losing the heel off his shoe one afternoon in an attempt to get out of the way of the Republican cavalry. During his days at the rue Monsieur le Prince, Antonio was altogether different from the gentle schoolmaster with whom the Bohemian Manuel is generally contrasted. He kept a revolver in his dressing-table and once drew it on an unfortunate tailor who had wanted him to pay his bills. After barely three months in Paris, Antonio decided to pack up and go home, leaving Manuel to carry on with the boring, poorly-paid job of translator alone.[1]

After his brother's departure Manuel penetrated further into the literary groups in Paris and counted among his friends the poet Jean Moréas, the essayist Ernest la Jeunesse, the dramatist Georges Courteline, the anarchist poet Laurent Tailhade, the exiled Oscar Wilde and the Russian Constantine Balmont. He was also introduced to André Gide and others by Paul Fort, and enjoyed the new sensation of being cosmopolitan, an epithet never more complimentary than at that moment and in that place.[2] He was

---

[1] Pío Baroja, *Desde la última vuelta*; I. López Lapuya, *La bohemia española en París a fines del siglo pasado* (Paris, 1927), p. 354.

[2] See *Unos versos*, pp. 52–5, and *El amor*, p. 71. Through la Jeunesse he later became a correspondent of *Le Journal*. While in Paris he translated and acted in a one-act play by Courteline which Courteline himself produced, presumably for the benefit of the Spanish colony (Narbona, 'El gran poeta'). Moréas, uncharacteristically open and human towards Machado, encouraged him to start writing poetry; and to Balmont Machado said he was indebted for the ability to begin. Professor Tzerbikov kindly tells me that he once took a book to Paris for Balmont in which Machado had written: 'Al gran poeta Constantine Balmont que me ha curado de mi mayor enfermedad de no poder escribir'. He did not say how the cure was effected. Balmont certainly did not influence him directly: the titles of some of their poems are the same ('Oasis', 'Smoke' and 'Antiphony' for example) but their themes and tones are quite different.

sponsored by Gómez Carrillo, only a year his senior but widely known in Paris. Manuel had met him soon after his arrival and through him Antonio had got to know the two figures he mentioned in his succinct autobiography: Jean Moréas and Oscar Wilde. Carrillo was described by Baroja, with some hostility, as a sort of amateur policeman who took charge of the Spanish writers who went to Paris in search of a living. But with his wit, prepossessing appearance and the prestige of having had innumerable duels and love affairs, and of knowing all the important French writers, he could afford to behave like a policeman as he presided over his *tertulia* in the Café Napolitain and taught Spanish émigrés how to drink absinthe.

For part of 1900, the year of the Paris Universal Exhibition, Machado lived in the mezzanine flat, 29 rue du Faubourg Montmartre, which Carrillo kept as a more or less open house for Spaniards and Latin Americans in Paris. There he met Rubén Darío and Amado Nervo who had both come to Paris for the Exhibition. On seeing Vázquez Díaz's portraits of Darío, Nervo and Carrillo years later, Machado was immediately reminded of the best moments of his life in Paris. Life at the flat in Montmartre, frequented by artists of all nationalities and rich with the scent of Carrillo's mistresses, seemed to him 'una bohemia sentimental y pintoresca, rica de ilusiones'. He shared a room with Darío; they drank together and even quarrelled over a woman from Montmartre, a dispute which Machado claimed would have estranged them had not Moréas settled the matter in a flood of champagne and poetry at a party in the Café Cyrano.[1] Much of

---

[1] 'Los buenos oficios del gran poeta Moréas, nuestro gran amigo y contertulio del Café Cyrano, nos pusieron en paz bajo un diluvio de champagne'; Manuel Machado, 'Rubén y Yo', *Arriba*, 5 February 1946. This article, written less than a year before Machado's death, cannot be accepted uncritically. For instance Machado says the year in question was 1898. However, all the evidence points to the year 1900. Darío himself was sure he had stayed at Carrillo's flat during that year (*La vida de Rubén Darío escrita por él mismo*, Barcelona, 1922, p. 229). Furthermore Amado Nervo was never in Paris before 1900, when he came as foreign correspondent of *El Imparcial* for the Exhibition and met many of the people Machado had met: Darío, Wilde and Moréas. And of course Machado himself elsewhere (*Unos versos*, p. 52) said he left for Paris in 1899. See also the accounts of his 'aventuras galantes' in *El amor*, and *El Liberal*, 3 June 1918 and

the golden light of this sentimental Bohemia may well emanate more from Machado's nostalgia in reminiscing than from the reality of the time. Nevertheless the air he breathed intoxicated him, just as it had intoxicated the Rubén Darío of *Los Raros*, and he captured their exotic world of ritual absinthes and Bohemian women in a verbal version of an Impressionist picture:

> Los placeres
> van de prisa:
> una risa,
> y otra risa
> y mil nombres de mujeres,
> y mil hojas de jazmín
> desgranadas
> y ligeras...
>
> Y son copas no apuradas,
> y miradas
> pasajeras,
> que desfloran nada más.   ('Encajes')

Poems like this one have deceived many critics into thinking that Machado's experience of Paris was superficial and transitory and that he was humanly incapable of having another sort of experience. L. A. Warren, for example, made this spiteful lunge at the Parisian Machado: 'In Paris, having no will-power, no energy and no interests, he became a follower of the fashionable decadent mode, slipped naturally into a refined sensualism, without apparently getting much pleasure out of it, only a vague sense of malaise and waste, and none of the pagan joy of Rubén Darío.'[1] Warren, like many other critics, was extracting biography from poetry, taking for lack of other evidence poems like 'Encajes' and of course 'Adelfos' as reliable accounts of Machado's activities in Paris. This sort of criticism is sufficiently unsophisticated to be

---

9 April 1919. When she heard of the plurality of her fiancé's affections, Eulalia Cáceres gave up writing. Amado Nervo mentions Darío, Gómez Carrillo, Moréas, Lola Noir and others, and describes incidents in which they were involved, in correspondence of this period (See Amado Nervo, *Obras completas*, Madrid, Aguilar, 1962, II, pp. 1136 ff.

[1] *Modern Spanish Literature*, II, p. 455, Cf. J. A. Balbontín, *Three Spanish Poets*, p. 114: 'Manuel amused himself with great abandon and fell in love with all the music hall artists who smiled at him'.

18

irrelevant to a literary study of Machado's poetry, but its pretensions to being biography remain. And so it is necessary to insist that unlike the imaginary aristocrat of 'Adelfos' and unlike those other Bohemians whose penury was an affectation, Manuel Machado had enough energy to work, and to complete a translation of the 400 pages of Paul Sébillot's *Contes bretons* for Garnier Frères.[1] Furthermore, to suggest that Machado had 'no interests' is absurd: as a citizen of 'la capital de nuestro siglo', as he called Paris, he discovered a new world of art, in Paul Fort and Lucien Guitry's experimental theatre, in the sets Aubrey Beardsley designed for Oscar Wilde's plays, and in the animated conversations about literature in which he participated. In Paris he learnt more about his craft as a poet than he did at any other time in his life. And in the relative tranquillity of the rue Vaugirard near the Luxembourg gardens, where he went to live by himself late in 1900, he gave proof of this when he composed the poems which later appeared in *Alma*. These poems show clearly the large extent to which he was influenced by writers he had met, and by a whole range of French poets from the Parnassians to the Symbolists.

Manuel Machado returned to Madrid in December 1900[2] a more mature writer and a changed man, to be welcomed now as an equal by the Spanish Modernists. As one who knew admired writers abroad and who could speak of contemporary artistic movements from personal experience, he became a close companion of the younger intellectuals in Madrid. The family flat in Fuencarral became a sort of Bohemian garret, frequented by Ramón del Valle-Inclán, Ramiro de Maeztu, Alejandro and Miguel Sawa, Rafael Cansino, José Ortiz de Pinedo, Bernardo G. de Candamo, Julio Pellicer, Francisco Villaespesa (at the forefront of every literary enterprise), and many others. He shared their poverty and their disdain for the *arribista* and displaying an arrogance worthy of the untamed Valle-Inclán he was once

[1] A rare book and, unlike Machado's later translations for Garnier, not listed in the catalogue of the Bibliothèque Nationale, Paris; which helps to explain A. McVan's puzzlement: 'So little did their work for the Garnier house interest the Machados that it remains vague just what they were doing. No book on which they worked has ever been named' (*Antonio Machado*, pp. 12–13).

[2] M. Pérez Ferrero, *Vida*, p. 60.

arrested with him in La Castellana for disturbing the peace.[1]
With his impatient wit he quickly became a valued spokesman
of the Modernists. Of his return to Madrid he wrote:

Vuelvo y todo está lo mismo, feo, triste.

....

'Modernista'—la palabreja es deliciosa. Representa sencillamente el último
gruñido de la rutina contra los pobres y desmedrados innovadores. De modo
que aquí no hay nada moderno, pero hay modernismo. Y por modernismo se
entiende...todo lo que no se entiende. Toda la evolución artística que de diez
años, y aún más, a esta parte ha realizado Europa, y de la cual empezamos a
tener vagamente noticia.[2]

Having now reason himself to decry the ignorance of revered
public figures, he participated actively in the Modernists' demonstrations against the literary and social establishment. After the
enthusiastic reception accorded to Galdós's anti-clerical play
Electra in January 1901, in some respects similar to that accorded
to *Juan José*, he played an important part in organizing the pro-
duction of the periodical named after the play, which began to
appear in March. Much of the discussion about policy took place
at Fuencarral, and Machado was elected to the editorial board
with Valle-Inclán, Villaespesa and Maeztu. José Machado has left
vivid memories of these discussions and reveals that during this
year of 1901 his older brothers were very close to Valle-Inclán and
Villaespesa, an association which had important literary consequences. He described them working together late at night:

En aquella estancia de la casa de los Poetas se veían a Manuel y Antonio y
con ellos a Valle-Inclán, delgado y doblemente pálido en contraste con su
negrísima barba y con un cuello de camisa alto, muy alto. También a Paco

---

[1] Ortega, 'Manuel Machado'; R. Cansinos-Assens (Rafael Cansino) quoted by
R. Gullón, 'Relaciones...entre Antonio Machado y Juan Ramón Jiménez'.
Before going to Paris Manuel Machado had admired only from a distance
'Valle-Inclán...el primero que sacó el modernismo a la calle' (*La Guerra
Literaria*, p. 29). The Modernists' sense of solidarity was due chiefly to a common
lack of public success: a rejection of a society which left them, in the words of
Pío Baroja, 'sin oficio, sin medios de existencia y sin porvenir'. Baroja con-
sideró que their Bohemianism was the result of 'el vacío hecho por los políticos
a todos los que no fueran sus amigos y quizá también por la pérdida de las
colonias, que, naturalmente, restringió el número de empleados en España'.
(*Obras completas*, v, pp. 578–9).
[2] *Juventud*, 10 October 1901.

Villaespesa, con su cara morena, sobre cuya frente le caía a un lado y a otro, de la partida raya, largos y desordenados mechones de su pelo negro. Antonio tenía puesto su largo y arrugado blusón de casa, y Manuel, que era el más friolero, estaba con una especie de pelliza, cuyo cuello tenía subido, y además se había puesto una gorra con visera negra de seda. Valle-Inclán acababa de leernos un trozo de un libro que estaba escribiendo entonces,...Pasada esta lectura, todos volvieron a adoptar las posiciones más usuales en que se ponían para continuar sus trabajos. Antonio, siempre insatisfecho, se le veía leer y volver a leer lo que estaba escribiendo. De cuando en cuando borraba algo y por encima escribía otra palabra...luego borraba otra vez. Villaespesa con la cara casi encima de sus cuartillas, parecía que estaba escribiendo con sus propios ojos enrojecidos y miopes. De cuando en cuando se animaba tanto que mojaba con redoblada fruición su pluma en el tintero una y otra vez. Manuel se cernía sobre el papel, pluma en mano, para caer con la palabra única, definitiva del final de alguna composición, o bien para escribir otra que abriese nuevos horizontes.[1]

Electra did not survive long, and was replaced in October by another periodical *Juventud*, in which Machado also had a large interest. A joint letter from him and Llanas Aguilaniedo to Miguel de Unamuno, in which Machado approached the older Unamuno with the familiarity of a fellow crusader, testifies that he was partly responsible for getting Unamuno to collaborate with them. The articles Machado wrote for *Juventud* were lively and savage. He was on sure ground. He exposed the inconsistency of the arguments used by the traditionalists against foreign innovations and concluded that his opponents were not so much old as worn out. He was prompted into a quick response by the speech of a former school friend, the sculptor Mariano Benlliure. On entering the *Academia de San Fernando*, Benlliure accused the Modernists of iconoclasm, irresponsibility and anarchism. In his defence Machado refused to believe that Benlliure could have written so absurd a speech alone and imagined it composed at a jolly party in the company of friends. This was his brisk summary of it: 'Ataques al modernismo, al impresionismo y a todos los en "-ismo" que esta gente tiene atravesados. Un finalito en pro de la eterna belleza, representada por los modelos académicos; loor a la disciplina...y Santas Pascuas.'[2]

Machado's arrogant defence of 'la poesía nueva' was justified at the beginning of the following year by his book *Alma*. The

---

[1] *Últimas*, pp. 63-4.   [2] *Juventud*, 10 October 1901.

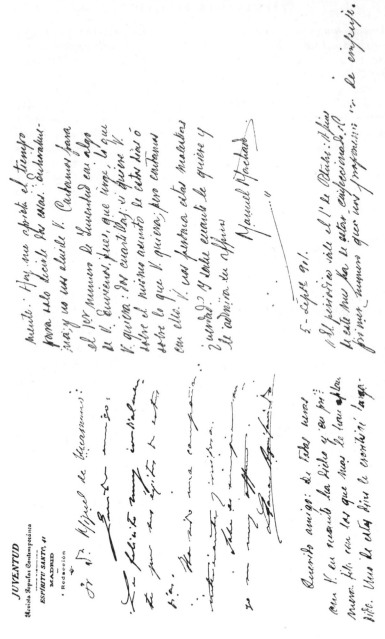

The joint letter in which Machado asked Unamuno to contribute to *Juventud*.

work contained a score of new poems written in Paris and Madrid, and those printed in *Electra*, slightly revised in some cases. Its publication passed unnoticed by the established critics of the time, but this was natural in so far as *Alma* was the work of a Modernist. Unamuno, however, devoted two columns of the *Heraldo de Madrid* to praise of Machado's book. He forestalled the attacks a normal reader could have been expected to make on the book by making them himself. To do so he personified himself as Brand, the hero of Ibsen's play, which he had just been reading; Brand the austere hero, obsessed with his mission as spiritual leader of his people. Some years later Unamuno referred to this personification in the prologue to *Alma. Museo. Los Cantares*, and again in a personal letter,[1] and said how deeply he had felt akin to Brand. Manuel was of course Brand's opposite in the play, Einar. For the purposes of his article, Unamuno made Machado's poetry the equivalent of Einar's lyrical speeches. He spoke of Machado, on the strength of the poem 'Adelfos' (dedicated to him), as a grasshopper who sang while the ant toiled. In view of the energy Machado was displaying at that time in literary campaigns of the sort for which Unamuno was himself becoming famous, this contrast was odd and even unfair,[2] though it was of course strangely prophetic. However, Unamuno concluded his article by paying Machado a high compliment, saying that his struggle with him had been salutary. He went further and claimed that Machado's verse was a necessary corrective to his own earnestness and he even admitted the dangers inherent in his pretensions to moral superiority. Offering his hand to Machado he exclaimed: 'Gracias hermano!'. There seems to be no reason to doubt that Unamuno was speaking the truth when he said on repeated

---

[1] From Salamanca, 26 December 1917; in the *BMB* and printed by A. Armas Ayala, 'Epistolario'.

[2] In the same way that the customary contrast between Modernist and *noventayochista* is odd, from the biographical point of view. Machado was neither more 'escapist' nor less socially aware than other regenerationists when, for example, he urged Unamuno to contribute something to an earlier review *España*, edited at the same address as *Juventud*, and like it, 'acomodada a las nuevas tendencias prácticas y reformadoras del alma moderna' and designed to 'educar al pueblo, a quien de preferencia va dirigida' (undated letter, Archivo de Unamuno, Salamanca).

occasions that his review of *Alma* was one of the most deeply felt he ever wrote. In his turn Machado was grateful to Unamuno for refusing to dismiss him as a poet of little or merely aesthetic consequence.

Unamuno's review enhanced Machado's reputation both among his friends and farther afield: Gómez Carrillo described *Alma* as the book Unamuno popularized. Within a few months another critic was considering Machado, on the strength of that book alone, as one of the two poets in Spain worthy of the name Symbolist. And Juan Ramón Jiménez, on his return to Madrid in 1902, spoke of Manuel and Antonio as 'mayores que nosotros en edad y todo, firmes sostenes de la *poesía nueva*'.[1]

For Manuel Machado himself, *Alma* was his first and best book. A few poems and dedications in it betrayed the survival of an attachment to his earlier literary environment and work: he continued to be the intimate of Calvo and Zayas for example.[2] But as a whole, with its ambitious formal and other innovations, the book was the product of a definitive experience, that of Paris, which cleanly divides two periods of his life. And this second period was characterized both by unprecedented poetic achievement and by a new vigour in criticizing a literature and a society which the Modernists considered to be narrow, Philistine and uninformed.

---

[1] Gómez Carrillo, *Mercure de France*, 4 April 1904, quoted by G. W. Ribbans, 'Unamuno and the younger writers'; Gonzalo Guasp, *Gente vieja*, 30 June 1902, quoted by G. Díaz Plaja, *Modernismo*, p. 38; J. R. Jiménez, *La corriente*, p. 67.

[2] 'Los inseparables de este momento somos Antonio y Manuel, el duque de Amalfi y yo'; R. Calvo reported by C. González-Ruano, *Las palabras quedan*, p. 344. The publication of *Alma* coincided with that of a collection by Calvo, *Evocaciones*, also printed by A. Marzo. Unfortunately, Calvo's desire to be a poet was greater than his performance as one: despite his good relations with the Modernists his verse did not escape the narrowest limits of the late nineteenth-century Spanish poetic tradition, and his book was quite eclipsed by *Alma*. The case of Zayas is slightly different. J. R. Jiménez assigned him an important role as an importer of books from France (Gullón, *Conversaciones*, p. 64), and the influence of the Parnassians is evident in his *Joyeles bizantinos*, which appeared three months after *Alma* and bore significant resemblances to it (see Chapters 9 and 11 below). Zayas made no formal innovations, however, a fact for which Benot was grateful in his review in *Los Lunes del Imparcial*, 21 and 28 July 1902. Manuel on the other hand became amusedly indifferent towards Benot, a revolutionary 'que no concebía que se hicieran revoluciones, después de la suya, ni en la Retórica' (*La Guerra Literaria*, p. 34).

3

A BOHEMIAN WINTER
(1902–1909)

La tragedia ridícula
de la bohemia... El mártir
que es un pobre, poeta de sus sueños,
y de sus realidades!...
— 'Invierno'

The Machado brothers both went back to Paris in the spring of
1902. They lived and worked separately, and from his flat in the
Boulevard des Batignolles Manuel travelled briefly to England
and Belgium before returning to Madrid at the end of the year.[1]
During their absence the atmosphere in the Spanish capital had
once again changed perceptibly. The enthusiasm of the days of
Electra and *Juventud* was, it is true, still evident in *Alma española,*
a new publication to which Manuel contributed articles in the
same satirical vein, as well as a passionate piece of 'social' writing
more characteristic of Dicenta than of a lyric poet ('El saber de la
miseria', December 1903).[2] And the inaugural session, at the flat in
Fuencarral, of the *Academia de la poesía española* (an iconoclastic
rival of the Real Academia) recalled directly similar scenes of 1901.[3]

[1] See Joaquín Machado, 'Relámpagos', and a letter to J. R. Jiménez from the rue
des Batignolles printed by R. Gullón, 'Relaciones... entre Juan Ramón Jiménez
y Manuel Machado'. Antonio, who again returned to Spain earlier than Manuel,
worked during the summer in the Guatemalan Embassy, a job arranged by Gómez
Carrillo. As for Manuel, many of the experiences recorded in *El amor* belong to
this stay in Paris, when he was, in his own phrase, one of the terrible 'españolos de
Batignolos' (*El amor*, p. 15). The journey to London suggests that the reference
to Whitechapel in the poem 'Internacional' could be autobiographical. Ricardo
Calvo claimed, in an interview recorded shortly before his death (*Ínsula,* 236–7,
p. 8), that on this occasion Manuel went to Paris as his guest and at his expense.

[2] Or of his companion Llanas Aguilaniedo, then famous for his 'exposures' of
working-class conditions in Madrid (see *La maia vida en Madrid,* Madrid, 1901).

[3] A leaflet, undated, in the *BMB,* reveals that Manuel Machado, Amado Nervo,
M. S. Pichardo, Pedro de Répide, Villaespesa, G. Martínez Sierra, M. de Val
and A. de Zayas were elected judges of 'un concurso de poesía dramática',
run by the *Academia de la poesía española*; see also José Machado, *Últimas,* p. 26.

But in fact by 1903 to 1904 the Machados' group was beginning to lose that dogged sense of solidarity which was well expressed by Antonio in a letter of this period to Juan Ramón Jiménez: 'Creo en mí, creo en usted, creo en mi hermano, creo en cuantos hemos vuelto la espalda al éxito, a la vanidad, a la pedantería, en cuantos trabajamos con nuestro corazón.'[1] It was a natural process. The thing that most held them together, their revolutionary aesthetics, became less and less important with the gradual acceptance of their ideas at all levels of literary life. Work by Modernists became the staple fare of readers of large commercial publications like *El Imparcial, Blanco y Negro* and *El Liberal*. Having spread himself on the sumptuous pages of *Blanco y Negro* in December 1903 with his poem 'Abel' and later with other poems and illustrated short stories, Manuel Machado no longer had any qualms, as he would have had three years previously, about offering dedications in *Caprichos* (1905) to newspaper bosses like M. de Cavia and Nilo Fabra. The Modernists' last show of solidarity was in effect their famous note of protest against Echegaray, and their battle with his protégé Ferrari, elected to the Real Academia in 1905. Academicians were the only prey left by this stage; otherwise the Modernists had won the day. Manuel Machado showed he realized this in an obituary of Navarro Ledesma, literary editor of *Blanco y Negro*, written the same year, in which he mentions Ferrari: 'Las firmas que han ilustrado el *Blanco y Negro* durante su direccíon prueban el ten con ten, que fue su misión, en el paso de *aquello* a *esto* en literatura. Martínez Ruiz figura al lado de Picón, Gómez Carrillo con Sellés, y yo junto a Ferrari o Grilo.'[2]

Once the struggle for recognition was over, the differences which separated the Modernists as artists began to seem more important than the cause which had united them. Manuel Machado's own horizon broadened generously to include very various features of the artistic life of Madrid of the time, a confused and animated world which still awaits a historian. He was equally well received among the two main groups the original

---

[1] 1903–4; quoted by R. Gullón, 'Relaciones...entre Antonio Machado y Juan Ramón Jiménez'.   [2] *La lectura*, v, 3.

Modernists split into, those presided over by Valle-Inclán in the Nuevo Café de Levante and Benavente in the Cervecería inglesa respectively; and he knew others less renowned, like Antonio Casero, Enrique Díez-Canedo, Manuel de Sandoval and José Almendros Camps, who could recite Verlaine and Samain by heart and whom Machado introduced to Darío.[1] Among the Latin Americans in Madrid he knew not only Darío, Nervo and Santos Chocano but others like the Mexican poet Joaquín Casasús and the two Argentinians José de Maturana and José Ingenieros whom Machado used to meet at the house of Cándida Santa María de Otero, with Villaespesa and Cristóbal de Castro;[2] Felipe Sassone, the Peruvian playwright, whom Machado had met in Paris in 1900 and who now accompanied him through the streets of Madrid: 'noctambulando en las calles céntricas, cenando en los "restaurants" de noche, frecuentando los salones y los saloncillos, formando parte de las peñas literarias y las tertulias artísticas, discutiendo en las redacciones y arreglando el mundo en los cafés...'[3] He knew newspaper men like Nilo Fabra, Pedro Penzol, Gómez Carrillo, Luis de Oteyza and Mariano de Cavia for whom he sometimes substituted in *El Liberal*;[4] bullfighters, especially Antonio Fuentes and Ricardo Torres;[5] artists like Julio Ruelas, Julio Romero de Torres and Juan Gris who illustrated Santos Chocano's *Alma América* (Madrid, 1906) and designed Machado's book plate and the cover for *Alma. Museo. Los Cantares* (1907) before going to Paris and becoming a Cubist. Machado used to meet Gris in the Café Oriental, just off the Puerta del Sol; that central area of Madrid was most beloved by

---

[1] M. Fernández Almagro, 'Juan Ramón Jiménez y algunos poetas andaluces'.

[2] In a letter to Machado, from La Plata, 12 October 1931, in the *BMB*, Cándida Santa María de Otero San Martín recalled the tertulias held in her 'histórica casita' opposite the Ministerio de la Gobernación over twenty years previously by Machado, Villaespesa, López Alarcón, Insúa, Castro, Maturana and Ingenieros. Machado dedicated 'Una pasion' 'Al admirable psiquiatra Dr. José Ingenieros' (*El amor*, p. 47).

[3] *Un año*, p. 47; see also F. Sassone, *La rueda de mi fortuna*, p. 306.

[4] See *El amor*, p. 204; Oteyza was a close companion later in *El Liberal* and *La Libertad* and, according to the prologue Machado put to Oteyza's *Obras completas* (Madrid, 1920), a friend since childhood.

[5] Antonio Casero said to me in a recent interview that Machado knew 'Bombita' intimately.

Machado and his companions, particularly the cafés Nueva
España and Candelas, where Machado was well known for his
sociability and his reluctance ever to be deprived of the attentions
of the women who frequented those cafés.[1]

The bookplate Juan Gris designed for *Alma. Museo. Los Cantares* in the Aubrey
Beardsley style which he abandoned almost immediately afterwards on going
to Paris.

From a literary and human point of view alike, the most distinctive and influential of Machado's many friendships were those
which linked him with Juan Ramón Jiménez and with Rubén
Darío. After their second visit to Paris, the Machado brothers fell
into the habit of visiting Jiménez in his retreat, the Sanatorio del
Retraído. Their relationship with him was never more robust
than (by his own account) his health was, but it was important.
Jiménez had returned from Paris even more recently than they,
bringing books with him and talking about French Symbolists
who were until then little known in Spain. The younger poet,
enthroned after 1903 on his self-consciously exclusive monthly

[1] R. Gullón mentions the Machado who was 'muy amigo del mujerío y la
tertulia' in *Conversaciones*, p. 42. Pedro Penzol also described him in a recent
letter to me and said that he first met him 'en compañía del pintor Juan Gris y
solíamos vernos en el café Oriental (si mal no me recuerdo) al lado de la Puerta
del Sol'.

MANUEL MACHADO ⋄⋄ ⋄⋄

⋄⋄ ⋄⋄ ⋄⋄ ⋄⋄ CAPRICHOS

LA HIJA DEL VENTERO

> «La hija callaba y de cuando en
> cuando se sonreia».—*Cervantes.*—
> *Quijote*

«La hija callaba
y se sonreía»...
Divino silencio,
preciosa sonrisa
¿por qué estáis presentes
en la mente mía?

La venta está sola.
Maritornes quiña
los ojos durmiéndose...
La ventera hila.
Su mercé el Ventero
en la puerta atisba
si alguien llega... El viento
barre la campiña.

Al rincón del fuego
sentada la' Hija,—
soñando en los libros
de Caballerías—

One of Machado's poems as it appeared in *Helios.*

29

Helios, exacted respect. Manuel had poems published in *Helios* and reviewed for it, but played a comparatively minor rôle in the venture as a whole. Aware of Juan Ramón's fastidious taste, he even apologized to him in advance for the superficiality of the poems which he was writing at the time and later incorporated into *Caprichos*.[1] He was spared for the time being the rigorous reappraisal undergone by the former hero and captain of the Modernists, Villaespesa, whom Juan Ramón began to treat with undisguised impatience. He was, however, refused the possibility of honouring Jiménez, as he offered to, with a dedication in the unfortunate collection *Caprichos*.[2]

Machado's friendship with Darío was altogether less anaemic and they continued to drink and philander in each other's company as they had in Paris. They met whenever Darío came to Madrid, and with Antonio Machado, Ricardo Calvo, the Sawa brothers and Amado Nervo withdrew to a favourite bar, the Café de Levante or another in the Calle de las Hileras. Manuel penetrated the intimacy of Darío's household, where he knew Darío's natural child 'Phocas el campesino' and fell in love with María Sánchez del Pozo, the sister of Francisca, Darío's mistress. The exclamatorily erotic poem 'Aleluya' in *Cantos de vida y esperanza* (1905), was the one poem Darío dedicated to Machado, and Machado reciprocated by offering the whole book *Caprichos* to Darío.[3] They shared not only literary taste and expertise but a whole attitude to life, a religion almost. In Machado's case this

---

[2] In a letter, Madrid, 30 January 1903, quoted by R. Gullón, 'Relaciones...entre Juan Ramón Jiménez y Manuel Machado'.

[1] On sending the manuscript of *Caprichos* to Juan Ramón on 15 July 1903, Machado wrote: 'Escoja una poesía para que lleve su nombre' (R. Gullón, *art. cit.*). It is interesting to note that already after the publication of *Soledades* (1902), Antonio's reputation began to increase, sometimes at the expense of Manuel's (who was nevertheless the first to sing his brother's praises). Manuel's friendship with Juan Ramón did not get off to a good start: sometime before his favourable review of *Rimas* in *El País* (1902), he had said of Juan Ramón: 'Para algunos es un simple neurasténico. Yo creo que es un simple simplemente' (R. Gullón, *art. cit.*).

[3] See José Machado, *Últimas*, p. 22; L. Granjel, *Panorama*, p. 81; A. Velasco Zazo, *Florilegio de los cafés* (Madrid, 1943), p. 94; M. Fernández Almagro, *Vida y literatura de Valle-Inclán* (Madrid, 1943), p. 109; and A. Oliver Belmás, *Este otro*, pp. 95, 202.

attitude, part of his attitude to Spain, was the first hint he gave of a faith which in the end made him more reactionary than those he criticized as a Modernist. In 'Despedida a la luna' he said he was no longer captivated by that other world of Paris:

> Dejé el vagar infeliz
> y la tristeza infinita
> de un vivir cosmopolita
> sin amparo y sin raiz
>
> por la ventura posible
> y por la dicha segura,
> y por la tibia dulzura
> de un amor más apacible.
>
> Volví de París, en fin,
> donde nos hemos querido,
> y he puesto ya en el olvido
> mis aventuras de Arlequín.

In fact, he went back again to France almost immediately after publishing this poem, but that does not prevent us taking his disenchantment with being cosmopolitan seriously. At best the problem was delicately stated and had two sides. On the one hand he had felt already in Paris that the image of Spain abroad was distorted; on the other he was not sure how far he could honourably identify himself with that part of Spain he thought was misunderstood. He described this indecision in detail and with great sensitivity in 'Noche de verbena', an essay published in *Los Lunes del Imparcial* in August 1904. More typically, *Amor al vuelo*, a play he wrote with Luis Montoto and had performed in Seville earlier in the year, bore no signs of such hesitation. Ricardo, the hero, a Sevillian who has spent some time in Paris, is cosmopolitan, agnostic and an advocate of free, enlightened relationships between the sexes; Soledad, his heroine, also strives to break traditional bonds. After making themselves ridiculous they realize their mistake, get married in church and symbolically throw all the French books they possess into the fire. Distrusting his own agnosticism, Machado sympathized at this time with the self-consciously Christian group formed by Darío, Nervo and Santos Chocano. The intensity with which he evoked the classic sinner-saint figure 'Don Miguel de Mañara' is powerful enough to make credible Juan Ramón's claim to have seen him dressed as a penitent of the Cofradía del Silencio in the Holy Week processions in Seville.[1]

The Bohemian and anarchic view of life which Machado held as a Modernist was, then, being compromised both by an admission that he had nothing new or challenging to say for the moment, and by fascination for a Spanish tradition he had declared stultifying. But he was goaded on, almost despite himself, during the next few years, to live out to the end, as few of his companions did, the 'tragedia ridícula de la bohemia'. The goad was, above all else, adverse criticism.

Caprichos and *La fiesta nacional* (1906) were well received by Darío,[2] and Martínez Sierra and Gómez de Baquero both showed an unbroken faith in the poet of *Alma* in their reviews of *Alma. Museo. Los Cantares* (1907). Other critics were less generous and some openly suggested that Machado was in decline. Manuel Abril wrote in *La Lectura* that since the struggle to establish new aesthetic values was no longer so fierce Machado was resting on his laurels, having given up the attempt to improve his own poetry. The best of the prologue Unamuno put to *Alma. Museo. Los Cantares* was a repetition of what he had said about *Alma*, and he hinted at the general indifference to Machado's poetry, suggesting, how ingenuously it is difficult to tell, that he should settle down and get married. While Villaespesa, referring to Machado as a collaborator in their review *Renacimiento*, would still include him among *the* poets in Spanish and equal to himself, Antonio Machado, Juan Ramón, Darío and Nervo, not long afterwards he confided to Juan Ramón that he thought that Manuel was finished

[1] *La corriente*, p. 43. An idea of the conscious Christianity of Darío's group can be gained from the dedications in Santos Chocano's *Alma América* (Madrid, 1906). 'Evangeleida' (p. 63), the poem offered to Darío, bore the following note: 'Dedico este poema cristiano a Darío, porque tanto Rubén como yo tenemos la osadía, en estos tiempos de indiferentismo, de creer públicamente en Dios'. 'El árbol bueno' (p. 166), the poem dedicated to Machado, was perhaps even more overtly Christian and began: 'Tuyo es ¡Señor! el numen que me inquieta, / tuya es ¡Señor! la fiebre que me abrasa'.
[2] R. Darío, 'Nuevos poetas de España' *Opiniones* (Madrid, 1920), p. 191 and 'La fiesta nacional', *Prosa dispersa* (Madrid, 1919), p. 47.

and impossible.[1] Echoing Clarín's damning remark about the two and a half poets of his age, Andrés González Blanco declared that the three and a half poets of his age were Antonio Machado, Juan Ramón Jiménez, Villaespesa...and Manuel Machado. He sent his condolences to the pale ghost of the poet who had written *Alma*. Much of González Blanco's criticism was stupidly unkind, but it was not isolated; and as if to lend weight to his essay he reported a telling remark Juan Ramón had made to him about *Caprichos*: 'Es una obra...que parece escrita por Fuentes'. Antonio Fuentes Zurita, Machado's great Sevillian bullfighter friend, a prodigious *banderillero* and *matador*, was the subject on whom *La fiesta nacional* was based and to whom it was dedicated. Juan Ramón remarked elsewhere on Machado's affinity to Fuentes, on the *banderillero's* delicacy Machado praised in lines that have often been quoted without due regard for his somewhat radical irony:

Prefiero
a lo helénico y puro lo *chic* y lo torero.

Y, antes que un tal poeta, mi deseo primero
hubiera sido ser un buen bandillero.   ('Retrato')

But it was not the delicacy that Juan Ramón meant on this occasion.

Machado responded to these unkind remarks with sham humility, saying that everybody was quite right in believing that he was finished. In what he called the 'Prólogo-epílogo' of his next book, which had the disarming title of *El Mal Poema*, he said he was content to have been nothing more than the favourite bard of courting couples:

Tal me dicen que fuí para ellos. Y tal
debí de ser. Nosotros nos conocemos mal
los artistas...Sabemos tan poco de nosotros,
que lo mejor tal vez nos lo dicen los otros...

He made the same point in the same ironic way by paraphrasing a remark which Zorrilla made as an old man and which Machado

[1] In two letters to J. R. Jiménez, Madrid, 17 July 1907 and Madrid, 29 October 1909, respectively, printed by R. Gullón, 'Relaciones literarias entre Juan Ramón y Villaespesa'. Those other reviews of Machado's books mentioned in the text can be found in the Bibliography under their authors.

admitted on another occasion (*La Guerra Literaria*, p. 21) to finding very moving:

> Ya estoy viejo y ya no valgo
> lo que han dicho que valía.

On Machado's lips it became:

> Ya estoy malo, y ya no bebo
> lo que han dicho que bebía.   ('Yo, poeta decadente')

In view of prevailing opinion he admitted that it would probably be better if he renounced his claim to the title of poet, taking the first of a long series of farewells from his public:

> Renuncio,
> pues, a ser un Verlaine, un Musset, un D'Annunzio,
> ⸺⸺⸺⸺
> Resumen: que razono mi *adiós*, se me figura
> por quitarle a la sola palabra su amargura.   ('Prólogo-epílogo')

He said goodbye elsewhere in the poetry he wrote between the years 1907 and 1909, and even in private letters. When sending Rubén Darío a copy of *Alma. Museo. Los Cantares* for instance, he said again: 'Esos versos son todo. Todo, por ahora, y quizás por siempre...'[1]

Despite all this verbal show of contrition, in deed Machado gave no indication whatsoever of wanting to give up his claim to being a poet. He published the very promises to stop publishing, as well as many other new poems, in national periodicals and the collection *El Mal Poema*. Perhaps the most striking proof of the danger of believing in Machado's professed lack of self-confidence as a poet is his refusal to take a regular job and thereby relegate his poetry to a place of secondary importance. Unlike his brother, for example (employed by the State as a school teacher from 1907), with a Modernist's distrust of the *arribista* Manuel Machado clung to the Bohemian ideal of an uncompromised poet, even though this meant living indigently (as his brother José saw) and working hard in a variety of unelevating capacities, mostly as a translator. He even asked Darío for money in return for doing occasional

---

[1] From a letter, 22 May 1907, printed by A. Ghiraldo, *Archivo*, p. 429.

clerical work in the Nicaraguan Embassy when Darío was ambassador there in 1908 and 1909.[1] The gulf between the ideal and the reality was for him ludicrously tragic:

> Y esta ancestral pobreza
> española del vate...
> La tragedia ridícula
> de la bohemia...   ('Invierno')

His consciousness of squalor and poverty, a deathly omnipresent disease which afflicted him and his companions alike, was powerfully expressed in the poems on the deaths of those companions ('A José Nogales, muerto', 'En la muerte de José Palomo Anaya') and on the appalling end of Alejandro Sawa ('A Alejandro Sawa, Epitafio'), blind, abandoned and penniless, in the winter of 1908–9, the finale of *Luces de bohemia*. And once again he taxed his society for being Philistine, this time not with prancing confidence but with bitterness:

> En un pobre país viejo y semisalvaje,
> mal de alma y de cuerpo y de facha y de traje,
> lleno de un egoísmo antiartístico y pobre
> —los más ricos apilan Himalayas de cobre,
> y entre tanto cacique tremendo, ¡qué demonio!,
> no se ha visto un Mecenas, un Lúculo, un Petronio—,
> no vive el Arte...O, mejor dicho, el Arte,
> mendigo, emigra con la música a otra parte.
>
>   ('Prólogo-epílogo')

Machado himself, in the words of the popular saying he was alluding to, went elsewhere with his music: back to Paris, to work again for Garnier Frères. Three of the books he translated were published in 1909; having to return, an older man, to the same translator's desk, caused him to deplore his ill fortune (in a some-

---

[1] D. Álvarez, 'Cartas inéditas'; José Machado, *Últimas*, p. 36. When recollecting this period Manuel said that the natural end of an independent poet was to die of hunger: 'De este modo, a menos de ser rico por su casa—rara avis—o de escapar a la miseria por una carrera facultativa seguida de una reñida oposición y que a menudo nada tenía que ver con las Musas, la muerte natural de todo poeta español era necesariamente de "hambre"' ('Manuel Machado habla de economía', *Estafeta literaria*, 10 October 1944).

what Olympian tone it is true) in 'La vie...', a sonnet written in French and published the same year;

> Je me suis arrêté à toutes les frontières
> et je n'ai pas goûté la paix d'un seul pays,
> la terre qui délasse ni l'eau qui désaltère.
>
> A attendre le soleil il s'est fané mon lys.
> J'arrive où l'on ne sait...Et, sur la fin, je vois
> qu'il faudrait parcourir la route une autre fois.

If he started off once again along the same road, this time it was without illusion. The Parisian atmosphere which had intoxicated him nine years earlier had palled: fashions had changed and even Jean Moréas looked old with his once impeccable cuffs frayed; a love affair was not an adventure but a stupid interlude between two working days worthy of no more comment than the slang word 'Chouette'. In his poetry Machado described himself as a lonely, unhappy man; Ramón Gómez de la Serna, who saw him sitting alone in a bar in the Boulevard Saint Michel, confirmed at least his uncharacteristic solitude:

> Alguna vez veía a Manuel Machado escribiendo en el café de abajo de mi hotel, en la Source, el café ideal para perder bien una tarde, es decir para perderla inmortalmente. Yo admiraba a Manuel Machado, pero no me acercaba a él respetando su soledad que él defendía tanto como yo la mía. No, yo no quería tampoco que nadie me perturbase en París, y menos los viudos de España.[1]

The quantity of verse Machado produced between 1907 and 1909 and the lengths to which he was prepared to go in order to be primarily a poet make it plain that he did not intend his renouncing that title to be taken at its face value. Moreover, many things suggest that the epithet 'Mal' in *El Mal Poema* was something more than ironic self-defence. As an apology for the breach of good taste, as he put it, which he had committed in composing the poems in that collection, Machado published a remarkable open letter to Juan Ramón Jiménez, then secure in his villa in Moguer.[2] He excused himself for offending his reader with his 'bad' poems but regretted that he could do no less than reflect some of the aspects of the environment he found himself reduced

---

[1] *Automoribundia*, p. 215.   [2] *La Guerra Literaria*, p. 117.

to and which Juan Ramón, with his private income, escaped. Some critics have been surprised that Machado should have adopted so apparently submissive a tone before the younger Juan Ramón and with their surprise have shown that Machado's finer irony evaded them. He was apologizing for *El Mal Poema* only in the best sense of the word and was not altogether sincere in lamenting that his verse did not range only over accepted poetic areas. On the contrary, he was making one of the first attempts in his language to create poetry out of that sordid city life by means of slang, sarcasm and deliberate prosaism. The dawn after a *juerga*; tired eyes, dirty hands and a bad taste in the mouth after a pointless night-long conversation in a café; a woman growing uglier in the early morning light and the dawn itself smiling and stupid like the face of a pregnant woman; all this, the more powerful element of his 'bad' poetry, was part of his experience during these years of penury. As a whole it represented a nightmare vision of the city in the mind of an overtired and ill man.[1] However Machado was not successful in maintaining or developing the intensity of the more expressive poems in *El Mal Poema*. This was because he wrote 'bad' poems for only a brief period, which ended abruptly in the radical change in his circumstances brought about by his marriage in 1910.

[1] Machado began *El Mal Poema* by announcing that the doctor had ordered him to give up writing. However, there is no direct evidence to prove that he was ill, apart from an occasional hint in the letters to Juan Ramón printed by R. Gullón, and the story 'La convalecencia' (*El amor*, p. 57), reprinted in the medical journal *Medicamenta*, 16 November 1946, as a case history. There, the vision of the city in the mind of a fevered man has the same grim quality it has in 'Yo, poeta decadente..', 'La canción del alba' and 'En la muerte de José Palomo Anaya'. Recognizing the originality in Spanish of *El Mal Poema*, Dámaso Alonso has compared the book to works by Baudelaire and Corbière ('Ligereza y gravedad'). This is valuable, but I think Machado also partakes of a tradition of poetry about Madrid slum life exemplified in works like *Los gatos* and *Los castizos* by Antonio Casero, a friend of Machado's and a disciple of López Silva. Unfortunately this tradition has received little or no critical attention.

4

'ARS MORIENDI'

(1909–1923)

Acabe—como mustias las flores, como exhausto
el arroyo, en la hora del pleno sol de estío —
la canción empezada al alba con el fausto
primaveral. Y sea éste el instante mío.

—'Piedra preciosa'

Manuel Machado's unsettled Bohemian life culminated in an
escapade to Barcelona in July 1909 in pursuit of Julia, a young
Catalan girl; Pérez Ferrero has described the circumstances surrounding the affair, Machado's acquaintance with Francisco
Ferrer and his experience of the Bloody Week in that city.[1]
Suddenly finding his situation ludicrous, Machado quickly moved
on again, on a ship to the south of France. In the poem 'Marina'
he wrote about the voyage and his own desire never to settle,
never to be bound to anyone or anything. Then, as if dissatisfied
with his dissatisfaction, he just as suddenly went back to Seville
and there married his cousin Eulalia Cáceres the following June.
A man in his late thirties, he thus honoured his promise to the girl
who had been, *de iure*, his fiancée for the previous thirteen years.
In a letter to Juan Ramón Jiménez of 1911 he described his new
household and his intention of forgetting his earlier life:

De mi vida.

Me casé, en efecto, hace poco más de un año, en Sevilla, con mi prima
Eulalia, mi amor de niño, mi primero y único amor verdadero. Lo demás no
han sido más que escarceos más o menos sensuales y correr del potro joven...
Me traje a mi mujer con mi madre y aquí vivimos contentos y felices, como en
el final de los buenos cuentos. Mi hogar es dulce y tranquilo, mi compañera
hermosa, buena y amante.[2]

[1] *Vida*, pp. 95–100; see also Machado's own remarks in *El Liberal*, 19 January
1918.
[2] Published by R. Gullón, 'Relaciones...entre Juan Ramón Jiménez y Manuel
Machado'.

Only his feelings for Eulalia could have led him to interpret so
gallantly Verlaine's attitude to Mathilde in 'La mujer de Verlaine',
written shortly after his own marriage: he forgot the mean side
of the story and imagined Verlaine yearning, in a foul-smelling
hotel in the Latin quarter of Paris, for a distant and ideally good
woman. Even in his most abandoned years Machado had always
sent an inscribed copy of his latest book to Eulalia and now, by
marrying her, finally shifted the emphasis in Darío's phrase: 'Mi
esposa es de mi tierra; mi querida, de París'.

Machado was the first to describe his marriage as a turning point
in his life. Nothing could be clearer than the contrast he made
between his Bohemian life and the peace of his new household.
Referring to the mood of *El Mal Poema*, he said: 'Esto es agrio,
duro, detestable. Todo lo cambió pronto la mano de una mujer
santa, llena de gracias y de gracia, que había sabido esperarme.'[1]
Their first-floor flat in Madrid, 20 Corredera baja de San Pablo,
was small, old enough to be historic and tastefully arranged with
furniture carved by Luis María Durán (an ancestor of Manuel's)
whose copies of Murillo adorned the walls. Eulalia, devout and
devoted, made fair copies of her husband's poems in her regular
hand and saw to his needs. Having deflowered his independence
he now dismissed it with a gesture of knowing complacency: 'Y
ser feliz y artista no lo permite Dios' ('La mujer de Verlaine').
And he allowed this mood to permeate his poetry in poems like
'Febrerillo loco' and 'A la tarde'. He reconciled himself to
society, not boycotting national poetry competitions, and being
asked in turn to give public lectures and poetry readings. In a talk
he gave in the Ateneo in 1911[2] he spoke so condescendingly of
Modernism as a thing of the past that he was criticized in the press
as 'un buen burgués'.

This was unkind, if only because Manuel Machado was enjoying
few of the social and financial advantages of being bourgeois in a
bourgeois society. The first years of his married life were pre-
carious. He found it necessary to keep working for Garnier

[1] *Unos versos*, p. 85.
[2] 'Los poetas de hoy'; commissioned, like 'El génesis de un libro' the following
year, by the Ministerio de Instrucción Pública, and published in *La Guerra
Literaria*.

Frères, and the tone of the letters he wrote to Rubén Darío enquiring about payment for the short stories he sent to *Mundial Magazine* makes it clear that he needed every peseta he could earn by his pen.[1] For with his new responsibilities and his nagging money problems he learnt for the first time how to exploit his writing consciously and consistently, notably in the volume *Cante hondo* (1912). Sensitive to the success of Rodríguez Marín's *Fiesta de la copla* held in the Ateneo in 1910, and of Villaespesa's book *Andalucía*, illustrated by Romero de Torres, which sold out the next year, Machado followed a trend and resurrected the 'popular' verse he himself had written and suppressed long ago, before going to Paris. He judged the occasion well and was not surprised when a thousand copies of *Cante hondo* were sold within twenty-four hours of appearing in the bookshops.[2] Before long he too was enlisting Romero de Torres's help in preparing a second enlarged edition.

But this was still not enough. Even with his various incomes as a writer, translator, public lecturer and part-time office worker in the *Junta de Iconografía Nacional*—a job gained through J. J. Herrero, an intimate of Canalejas[3]—he found difficulty in keeping himself, his wife, his mother and his flat. He decided at last to get a permanent job, consummating an attachment he had resisted for so long. Almost as if to atone for the excesses of his Bohemian life he chose the proverbial seclusion and regularity of the librarian's existence. To do this and to enter the *Cuerpo facultativo de Archiveros, Bibliotecarios y Arqueólogos*, he needed a further University degree, and during the summer of 1912 he studied archaeology, medieval bibliography, vulgar Latin and other subjects at the Universidad Central. In April he explained to Juan Ramón that

---

[1] See two letters from Madrid of November and December 1911 published by D. Álvarez, 'Cartas inéditas'.

[2] M. Pérez Ferrero, *Vida*, p. 106.

[3] P. de Répide, 'Lira y guitarra'; he used the *Junta's* paper for private correspondence and the photographic service to illustrate *Apolo*. The—remote—connection with Canalejas (whose assassination in 1912 moved him deeply) did not involve any exclusive political sympathy; for the same year he took the extraordinary step of dedicating *Trofeos* to Maura 'en homenaje de admiración y respeto', when Maura's name was still anathema after the Bloody Week in Barcelona. (See also a letter from Maura, Palma de Mallorca, 8 February 1912, in the *BMB*).

that was why he had little time to write poetry: 'Pero habrá que esperar—por eso mismo—a que yo me deshaga de una serie de pequeñas ocupaciones y molestias de asuntos que me quitan el tiempo.'[1] In November he announced to Darío that he had completed his university courses, cynically apologetic about his efforts to become a Civil Servant: 'Este verano ha sido para mí de trabajo, aunque no literario. He terminado la carrera de Bibliotecario y Arqueólogo, para tomar parte en las próximas oposiciones de febrero. He *hecho* un gran estudiante y tengo muy buenas esperanzas de obtener mi plaza. Une petite sinécure!'[2]

He applied to sit the *oposiciones* in February 1913, and on being appointed a third grade official of the *Cuerpo facultativo* in July, at 3000 pesetas a year, he was posted to Santiago de Compostela as a University librarian. The thought of being cut off from life in the capital distressed him, and for some time he stayed on in Madrid. He was at last persuaded to go to Santiago at the end of the year by a batch of exasperated letters, but he managed to arrange a transfer to Madrid almost immediately and returned to work in the Biblioteca nacional and some time later in the Biblioteca municipal where he remained for the rest of his career as a librarian.[3]

Machado accepted calmly the limitations and the advantages of being a civil servant. Occasionally he regretted the lost fire and freedom of his youth but, secure in his 'sinecure', for the most part

[1] R. Gullón, 'Relaciones...entre Juan Ramón Jiménez y Manuel Machado'.
[2] A. Ghiraldo, *Archivo*, p. 430. Machado's confidence was in part due to the fact that Rodríguez Marín was president of the examining tribunal. At Manuel's request Rodríguez Marín had, the previous September, ensured that Antonio got his job in Baeza after Leonor's death, when Giner, to whom Manuel had also appealed, had ironically not been able to help. (See a letter from Giner, 1 September 1912, in the *BMB*; P. Répide, 'Lira y guitarra' and E. de Las Navas, 'Manuel Machado ha cumplido 70 años'). The help Rodríguez Marín afforded both the Machados, out of respect for their father, can be understood only in terms of personal relationships, since, as is well known, Rodríguez Marín and Menéndez y Pelayo were hostile to Giner and the *institucionistas*, seeing Maura as their champion against Krausist influence in general (cf. *Biografía y epistolario íntimo de don Francisco Rodríguez Marín*, ed. J. Fernández Martín, Madrid, 1952, p. 162 ff.).
[3] Details of Machado's career as a librarian are taken from the file under his name in the Ministerio de Educación Nacional, Madrid.

that his reviews were ridden with kind clichés, Gómez Carrillo leapt publicly and effectively to his defence; and in a private letter compared his style to that of their common friend Catulle Mendès of *Le Journal*: 'Mi orgullo consiste en haberlo adivinado cuando usted mismo dudaba de llevar dentro un crítico a la parisiana, un hijo de Catulle Mendès.[1]

Towards the end of 1917 Machado was invited to write, in addition to his drama criticism, a weekly column of general comment on political and social events; he accepted and, occasionally interrupted by the censor, produced his 'Día por día de mi calendario', which José illustrated with his drawings. He had hardly completed this series of articles at the end of 1918 when he began another, 'Intenciones'. Shortly after the war the paper sent him abroad as a correspondent: officially on sick leave from the library, he toured Belgium and spent a pleasant spring in Paris where he renewed old friendships on more equal terms. He arranged to translate Descartes for Garnier, lunched with Georges Courteline, saw a rehearsal of Sacha Guitry's *Pasteur* in which his friend Lucien acted, dined with Fermin Génier, André Antoine, Carlos de Batlle and the Coquelins, shook hands with the Prince of Wales in the Palace Dufayal, conversed with Foch and spent an evening with Jaime de Bourbon and the Infanta Eulalia.[2]

During these years of success as a journalist, Machado came close to realizing the ambitions he betrayed when using the name of his ancestor the Marquis of Montevelo as a pseudonym. He was famous and lived well. Enveloped in the dark green cape Gómez Carrillo sent him from Seville when honeymooning there with

---

[1] From a letter headed 'Association des correspondents de guerre de la presse étrangère, 10 Rue de la Castellane, Paris' and dated 12 October, in the *BMB*. On occasions Machado was provoked into defending himself: 'Esta crítica se encara conmigo y me pregunta, de mal humor, porqué no declaro de un modo absoluto y categórico la maldad o la bondad de las comedias que reseño en mis artículos. Para que se enteren de una vez estos ansiosos de los porqués, les respondo: 'Porque ni esa bondad ni esa maldad existen. En cuanto a mi impresión, a mi opinión, si ellos no la advierten clara a través de mis crónicas..., ciego es el que no ve por tela de cedazo' (*El Liberal*, 5 February 1917).
[2] See the 'Crónicas de París' which he sent to *El Liberal* every few days from 25 February to 14 April 1919.

Raquel Meller, he was a well-known figure in the embassies and more expensive hotels and restaurants of Madrid; the Ritz, the Palace, Kutz, Echegaray and La casa Llardy.[1] He fraternized with the celebrities of the moment, some of whom, like Mariano Benlliure, he had attacked bitterly as a young man. He entertained Maeterlinck and Georgette Blanc during their visit to Spain and organized a series of parties for his heroine Sarah Bernhardt.[2] His signature appeared in Froilán Turcios's *La Esfinge*, Carrillo's *Cosmopolis*, Gershberg's *Observando España*, in *Letras*, *La Lectura*, *América latina* and a host of other reviews, all within the space of a few years. Editors pressed him with offers to publish his newspaper articles and poems in popular editions. As a public personality, Antonio Machado paled beside his brother: Gerardo Diego tells the revealing anecdote of how Antonio, a humble teacher of French in the provinces, was approached by someone at a local *peña* who said: 'Pero don Antonio, qué callado se lo tenía usted. Nos hemos enterado de que es usted hermano de Manuel Machado, el que escribe en *El Liberal*.'[3]

While Antonio was studying at the University of Madrid in 1917 and 1918, the brothers shared a house in General Arrando 4; José has described how the three of them spent winter evenings around the *camilla* after a walk in the northern outskirts of Madrid.[4] Antonio had a *tertulia* in the Café Español and Manuel would join the few who attended it before escaping, as Gómez de la Serna put it, 'hacia el barrio de la cuchipanda'.[5] Despite their mutual affection, the habits of the two brothers differed palpably. Manuel lived as glittering a life as his fame allowed him. He hankered after the pleasures of Paris and was invited to 'El Mirador', the villa Gómez Carrillo kept in Nice with Blasco Ibáñez, Maeterlinck and Max Regis as neighbours and which he described as:

[1] See letters from Carrillo (February 1920), J. Villardo (May 1921) and J. Chabás in the *BMB*; also Oliver, 'La capa de Machado', *Unión de Sevilla*, 8 January 1920, Villaespesa's poem 'La Maison Dorée'; and Machado's own article in *El Liberal*, 3 May 1918. The Marqués de Montevelo was a Portuguese nobleman who stayed faithful to Philip IV during and after the Portuguese rebellion of 1640; see P. de Répide, 'Lira y guitarra'.
[2] See *El Liberal*, 11 and 13 December 1916, and *La Libertad*, 14 May 1921.
[3] 'Manuel Machado'.   [4] *Últimas*, pp. 49 and 89.
[5] *Nuevos retratos*.

'una casita de canónigo italiano, con un jardín lleno de naranjos y una habitación amueblada con regalos de Maeterlinck y Max Regis'.[1] Manuel enjoyed the luxury of a country house himself; during his weekends there he wrote of the delights of summer evenings, of the eucalyptus at his window, the garden stream, the pine woods, the wheat fields and the peace of the countryside in poems like 'Paisaje' and 'Regreso'.[2] He even planned a holiday in Mexico with Carrillo and a certain 'don Hydrógenes' but Carrillo, finding the idea to his financial disadvantage, intimated that Machado was really better off at home with his wife in the flat they had just bought in Madrid. Machado's income as a journalist and his greatly increased salary as a librarian meant that he was relatively unaffected by the economic crisis of 1917 and could afford to become the owner of an apartment at 15 Calle Churruca where he and Eulalia remained for the rest of his life in Madrid. He furnished the flat well and, as before, copies of Murillo adorned the walls. Díez-Canedo bore in mind the luxury of Manuel's new home and the poverty of Antonio's when he said of 'Los dos hermanos poetas' at this time:

> Ya tienen hecha su obra, construida su casa. La del uno frente a los anchos campos de Castilla, sola en el páramo, con la musicalidad del viento en los chopos y el golpeteo de la lluvia en los cristales. La del otro, más complicada, en plena ciudad, con salones lujosos, muebles, tapices, alfombras, buenos cuadros, y, en el centro, un patio andaluz en donde se oye, a menudo, el rasguear de las guitarras.

The distinction between the two brothers had by now become commonplace in social and regional terms, but not in moral ones. Manuel no less than Antonio was considered a son of the *Institución libre*, and they both enjoyed close relations with the *Residencia de estudiantes*, which published his *Poesías completas* at the same time

[1] From a letter headed 'El Mirador, Chemin de Brancolar, Nice' s.d. (1922–3), in the *BMB*.

[2] See also 'Soledades' and 'Oleografía' in *Ars moriendi*. I have been unable to discover where Machado had his house but there can be no doubt that he had it, despite Pérez Ferrero's silence on the matter, for Carrillo referred to it in his letters and offered to send something to adorn the study: '¿Cómo va esa casita de campo? Algo tengo yo que mandar para adornar su despacho' (from a letter headed 'Redacción de *El Liberal*', s.d., in the *BMB*).

as Antonio's.[1] Despite his journalist's popularizing and plausibility he still had some credit as an intellectual. With the triumph of the Allies' cause he regained some of the ground he lost in the eyes of Ortega (who stated an early preference for Antonio)[2] and his group, when unlike Antonio he had declined to join the *Liga de educación política española*. And his supporters, if few, were powerful: as he said of Unamuno's favourable review of *La Guerra Literaria:* 'Esto me honra, me encanta y me da gran valor y virtud. Ya ve lo que digo de la crítica española: es más negada que el propio vulgacho. Y yo tengo cierto derecho a quejarme de la general incomprensión.'[3] Furthermore, as a poet he won renewed respect towards the end of this period of his life, on the strength of a few new and remarkable poems. Encouraged by Jorge Guillén he wrote for *Alfar*, the review founded by Julio Casal in Corunna in 1920; and unlike Villaespesa, Martínez Sierra and other contemporaries he was asked by Juan Ramón to contribute to *Índice* the following year. Machado (now on 'tú' terms with Jiménez) produced some poems which, free from the superficial Andalusianism of his newspaper verse collected in *Sevilla y otros poemas* (1919), withstood comparison with contributions by his brother, Moreno Villa, Jorge Guillén, García Lorca and Ortega. These poems were placed on the first pages of *Ars moriendi* (1921), a book warmly reviewed abroad, and in Spain by Gómez de Baquero and Jorge Guillén. In another farewell to poetry and life

---

[1] This edition, which I have not seen, is unmistakably among the 'obras publicadas' listed on the back covers of the Residencia's other editions of 1917. Machado lectured at the Residencia (see J. Moreno Villa, *Vida en claro*, p. 105) and on their behalf, for example at the Real Cinema on 14 December 1924 on the discovery of Tut Ankh Amen's tomb.

[2] In his review of *Campos de Castilla*, *Los Lunes del Imparcial*, 22 July 1912.

[3] In a letter s.d. (December 1913), headed 'Biblioteca de Filosofía y Letras' from 'Corredera baja 20 pral., Madrid' in the *Archivo de Unamuno, Salamanca*. Machado had sent the book to Unamuno with some trepidation: 'Bajo una apariencia banal y desarticulada es muy hondamente personal ese libro: es muy mío y temo que no se enteren de que hay en él puesta una gran cantidad de alma. Vea usted si vale la pena de que usted (quizá el único que sabía verlo) se lo diga a las gentes. Le recomiendo—sobre todo—la sección llamada 'Intenciones" (from a letter from Madrid, 6 December 1913, *ibid.*). Unamuno announced his intention of reviewing the book in 'Otro arabesco pedagógico', *Los Lunes*, 22 December 1913, before publishing his flattering 'Manuel Machado y yo' a fortnight later in the same newspaper.

Machado momentarily rediscovered the depth of *Alma* and *El Mal Poema*. As on previous occasions, his good-bye did not mean withdrawal and he continued to write poems for the daily newspapers. However, perhaps that was the point he was insinuating, that *Ars moriendi* was the last serious poetry he felt he could utter. In the midst of success and luxury he turned aside for a moment to commiserate with his mistresses for the skilful sterility of their love-affairs, and in the diamonds they wore he saw a cruelly perfect crystal, formed in a once fertile soul, which reflected in its facets a dead landscape and his frozen love ('Piedra preciosa'). As a young man he had deplored, with some wit, 'la santa fecundidad nacional, que infecta las calles de chiquillos';[1] but the tone of the talks he gave to children as a man approaching his fifties, and the tenderness inspired in him by the faces of children enchanted by a Christmas pantomime in December 1918,[2] suggest that he regretted his own childlessness in the way he regretted his failing creativity as a poet.

[1] 'Madrid, día por día', *Juventud*, 4 (30 October 1901).
[2] *El Liberal*, 31 December 1918; see also the beginning of his lecture to schoolchildren on *La vida es sueño* (2 December 1918), Madrid, Imprenta municipal, 1918.

5

ALLEGIANCE AND WITHDRAWAL
(1923–1936)

En medio del amor, de la ambición y el miedo
la música no más logra tenerme quedo.
—'Nuevo auto-retrato'

Manuel Machado's reaction to Primo de Rivera's coup d'état in September 1923 could easily be seen as nothing but cynical acquiescence, the tact of another Vicar of Bray. However, despite the ease with which Machado may have accommodated himself to subsequent regimes in Spain, despite the facile nihilism of so much of his writing, on this occasion at least some further reason must be sought for his political behaviour. Once he had forgotten the Bohemian anarchism of his youth he generally styled himself as a Liberal. Indeed when writing for *El Liberal* he showed a then understandable disgust with the 'panacea universal' of Bolshevism and a corresponding faith in the liberal democracy professed by the victorious Allies of the first world war. But on two issues he was more guarded: his concern with the ineffectuality of the Spanish parliament and his ambiguous attitude towards the trade unions, in his column *Día por día*, even earned him the wrath of the censor. His misgivings and the fierce pressures of the moment combined to make him break with *El Liberal* during the printers' strike of 1919, and ally himself, in word and deed, with the trade unions. Gómez de la Serna, who joined *El Liberal* in the autumn of 1919, described the rebellion of Machado and his companions in a detailed if somewhat dramatic way. Shortly after joining the staff of the newspaper he went to a party, in the cellars of a café in Madrid, given in honour of the theatre critic, at that time Manuel Machado, although Gómez de la Serna did not mention him by name. In the course of the party he became aware of a conspiracy to break away from *El Liberal* by striking in sympathy with the workers and founding a new paper *La*

Libertad. Faithful to the Liberal principles of his family and deeply hurt by the death of Miguel Moya not long after the new paper was founded, Gómez de la Serna took an almost apocalyptic view of that party in Machado's honour. He spoke of Moya as a martyr to a new generation of ruthless demagogues and thought the foundation of *La Libertad*, in December 1919, as important an event in Spanish history as the loss of the Philippine Islands: 'Recuerdo aquella tarde en toda su paturencia gris, día de naciencia de la importancia de los osados. Giró en aquel banquete la historia de España, otra historia como la de la pérdida de las Filipinas'.[1] The conspirators, Luis de Oteyza, Antonio de Lezama, Antonio Zozaya, Pedro de Répide, Manuel Ortiz de Pinedo, Manuel Machado and others, broke with Moya because they disagreed with his policy of 'sindicalismo nunca, sindicación patriarcal sí!';[2] they founded *La Libertad* in particular protest against the widespread lock-outs, supported by *El Liberal*, during the wave of strikes in 1919. These strikes were generally recognized as a result of the severe inflation of the time, and, less directly, as repercussions of the revolution of October 1917 in Russia and of the quixotic and unsettled hope that the catastrophe of the world war would herald a new and different society, a hope Machado evidently shared when he wrote of the collapse of 'el viejo mundo, basado sobre la fuerza, gobernado por instituciones que no comprendemos ya, plagado de anacronismos en descomposición deletérea, inútiles y perjudiciales, verdaderos cadáveres insepultos del poder absoluto, de la gloria militar, del fanatismo religioso, del imperialismo, de la teocracia, de la aristocracia hereditaria.'[3] A clear statement of policy was made in the first issue of *La Libertad* where the Spanish socialists were chided for being reluctant to join the Third (Bolshevik) Inter-

[1] *Automoribundia*, p. 319.
[2] This cry of Moya's was repeated loudly in *El Liberal* when it reappeared after the strike on 16 December 1919, sadly depleted by the loss of the conspirators who had refused to accept the pay rise offered on 8 December, when the strikes began, until the workers had also had their demands satisfied. On the first anniversary of *La Libertad*, 14 December 1920, its founders recalled that the paper had been born out of 'un generoso y bravo movimiento de emancipadora solidaridad, sentido y consagrado por un núcleo de escritores de la izquierda'.
[3] *El Liberal*, 4 November 1918.

Libertad

se ha
les de
el tor-
orrible
aación-
s des-
es pla-
un ser
e con-

torno
e una
poral-
te por
nares,
a vez
nal no

nación
idades
l mun-
o des-
, y la
Todas
n sido
tración
a ver-
rte co-
el de-
os or-

cues-

men de arrojar lejos de su lado aquello que es sangre de su propia sangre, no merece aspirar en la vida a las nobles prerrogativas del ser humano.

Gloriosa es la fecundidad, pero no para producir miserables y víctimas. Como un nuevo Moloch, aparece esa terrible institución oficial que ha devorado tantas existencias inocentes. Y el monstruo fatídico no es tan culpable como quienes arrojan el abundante y tierno pasto a su feroz voracidad El cierre del torno de la Inclusa debe ser, en efecto, definitivo. Castigados el aborto y el infanticidio, y, acabado aquel procedimiento para prescindir del hijo, quienes traigan nuevos seres a este mundo sabrán que se cuentran en el deber de criarles y de educarles, sin prostituir, enlodar y ensangrentar la que debe ser augusta misión de la maternidad.

PEDRO DE REPIDE

La Redacción de LA LIBERTAD está formada por Luis de Oteyza, Director; Antonio de Lezama, Redactor-jefe; Alejo García Góngora, Secretario de Redacción; Antonio Zozaya, Luis de Zulueta, Augusto Barcia, Pedro de Répide, Manuel Machado, Maximiliano Miñón, Alejandro Pérez Lugín, Ezequiel Endériz, Ricardo Marín, Francisco Hernández Mir, Ricardo Hernández del Pozo, Luis Salado, Manuel Ortíz de Pinedo, Víctor Gabirondo, Heliodoro Fernández Evangelista y «Alfonso», ex-redactores de **El Liberal**

Los poetas del día

A una marquesa

Tu boca, cuando me besa,
en repetirme se obstina
que vienes en línea expresa
de una elegante marquesa
que murió en g uillotina.

Socialismo moderado

Comentarios al Congreso socialista : : : : : :

La substancia de los partidos socialistas reside en el internacionalismo. El famoso imperativo de Carlos Marx gritando a la faz de la Humanidad: «¡Trabajadores del mundo, uníos!», ha sido la más rica prenda doctrinal del socialismo. A partir de ahí, todos los esfuerzos del proletariado han ido a unificar el pensamiento del universo obrero... Y de aquí nacen la Primera, la Segunda y, por último, la Tercera Internacional.

Ayer se discutió en el Congreso socialista que se está celebrando en la Casa del Pueblo este importantísimo tema. Se trató de adherirse a la Tercera Internacional o de quedar adheridos a la Segunda. Ello implica tanto como saber el espíritu revolucionario de un partido organizado para la revolución.

Daniel Anguiano, el ex diputado socialista, sostuvo la proposición de que el partido se adhiriera a la Tercera Internacional. Esta adhesión era el bolchevikismo, el sovietismo. La apoyó García Cortés con una documentación amplia y serena, haciendo un análisis perfecto de la Revolución rusa. Rusia—decía García Cortés—no es el desorden, no es la disolución. Rusia es el máximo de una conquista, el derecho íntegro del proletariado en el Poder, Indalecio Prieto, Julián Besteiro y otros significados congresistas defendieron la tendencia opuesta.

Y llegó la hora de votar. Mil votos, dos mil, tres mil... La mayoría fué los moderados, y el partido socialista español quedó adherido a la Segunda Internacional.

El caso es curioso. Los partidos socialistas de todo el mundo van delineando actitudes, definiendo doctrinas favorables a la Tercera Internacional. Ahí está Italia, que de una vez se suma a esta tendencia bolchevikista. Pero llega a España la hora de definirse, y el socialismo español, excesivamente menguado desde la pasada huelga general, se pronuncia casi en contra a todo el socialismo mundial. Los minoritarios están pasando a ser mayoritarios, y viceversa, en el Universo entero. Solamente en España se cree en aquel socialismo a lo Vanderbilt...

A section of the front page of the first number of *La Libertad* showing the list of collaborators and the beginning of the favourable commentary on the Third International referred to on p. 50.

4-2

national. The paper soon became less revolutionary but continued to support the cause of the trade unions and the radical educational reforms proposed by Santiago Alba.[1] Machado acted as both political commentator and theatre critic for *La Libertad* as he had done for *El Liberal*; it is important to emphasize this, since in later life he denied having written anything but theatre criticism.[2] In fact, shortly after the foundation of the new paper he attacked the Federación Patronal and thus adopted a very different attitude from the one he had adopted in the poem 'La huelga', written in defence of the Liberal industrialists during the general strike of 1917. In December 1919 he wrote: 'La Federación Patronal, dirigiéndose a los obreros, les quiere convencer, amablemente, de que su "Destino" no es otro que el de obedecer, sufrir, callar y arrimar el hombro. Que esa ha sido su misión hasta aquí es muy cierto; pero convertirla en Destino nos parece un poco arriesgado.'[3] In Machado's case, this un-Liberal sympathy with the trade unions was coupled with a failing faith in the viability of the party system in Spain. Already in July 1919 he had enthusiastically approved the dissolution of all political parties in Puente Genil and the setting up of a 'popular' directorate in their place.[4] By 1922 he warned that time was running out:

Los centros de la influencia social se han desplazado de algún tiempo a esta parte, buscando...los focos de la vida nacional, la cual, de espaldas muchas veces al rancio politiqueo—y a pesar de él—, crece, y prospera, y se fortalece.

[1] Carrillo, who remained with *El Liberal*, wrote to Machado in 1920: 'Por Gabriel España me he enterado de que el periódico de ustedes marcha viento en popa y de todo corazón lo celebro por Santiago Alba, por usted y por Lezama' (letter dated Montevideo, 29 October, in the *BMB*). In another letter of the same period (s.d. in the *BMB*) Carrillo revealed the extent of Machado's sympathy with S. Alba, who was the leader of the 'izquierda liberal' in opposition, by remarking: 'Usted ha sido siempre albista ardiente aun en épocas en que a algunos jefes de usted les chocaba y les disgustaba ese sentimiento'.

[2] 'Pasé luego a *La Libertad*, de la que soy redactor fundador y donde continué, haciendo exclusivamente la crítica dramática' (quoted by G. Diego, *Antología*).

[3] 'Intenciones', *La Libertad*, 31 December 1919.

[4] 'En Puente Genil se han disuelto todos los partidos y se han nombrado plebiscitariamente un directorio para defender los intereses de la población. Cuando todos los pueblos de España hayan hecho lo mismo, vendrán a los escaños del congreso y senado los verdaderos representantes del país' (*El Liberal*, 11 July 1919).

Se hace ahora muchas veces la verdadera política fuera de la esfera oficial, coincidiendo con las aspiraciones y necesidades del país. Unas Cortes que no sigan ese movimiento de aproximación, de adaptación, de consubstanción con las realidades vitales de España, no serán absolutamente nada.[1]

Whatever other motives Machado may have had for abandoning his Liberalism and welcoming Primo de Rivera, there can be no doubt that his hopes were raised by the Dictator's promise to rid the country of the abuses of the party system and his development of the 'sindicatos libres'.[2]

Within two years of Primo's assumption of power, Manuel Machado was appointed Jefe de investigaciones históricas, Director of the Biblioteca municipal and then Director of the Museo municipal, promotion which gratified his highest professional ambitions. Belying once more the nonchalant Sevillian, Machado was efficient and hard-working in his job: availing himself of the archives at his disposal he continued to produce learned articles, for the *Revista de la Biblioteca, Archivo y Museo* which he had founded with Ricardo Fuente, the previous Director, in 1924. At the time his appointment was criticized as irregular although he made no attempt to defend himself, unlike Antonio after his unconstitutional election to the Real Academia in 1927 as an opponent to the anti-Primo candidate Niceto Alcalá Zamora.[3] As long as six months before he was appointed Director Manuel Machado received requests for favours and *enchufes* on the assumption that

[1] From an article entitled 'Del natural' pasted in a scrapbook, in the *BMB*; underneath it there is a note in Machado's hand: 'Este artículo se publica en 1922. En 1923 vino la Dictadura de Primo de Rivera. Y tras ella todo lo demás hasta hoy—1946 Nove.'. A curious and significant attempt at self-justification.

[2] See Gerald Brenan, *The Spanish Labyrinth* (Cambridge, 1943), pp. 76–7, 84.

[3] 'El general Primo de Rivera, entonces jefe del Gobierno, dio una fiesta andaluza en honor de ellos, y poco después hizo a Antonio académico de la Española. Es el caso único de ser un escritor elegido para la Academia, sin haber propuesto su candidatura' (P. de Répide, 'Lira y guitarra'). Although J. Sampelayo reported that Manuel Machado had been elected 'tras un duro concurso' ('M.M. en su jubilación'), he was appointed 'sin votación' according to a note on his retirement from the *Cuerpo facultativo*, 31 July 1925, in the Archivo del Ministerio de Educación. Astrana Marín cast suspicion on the circumstances surrounding the appointment in *El Diario del pueblo*, 16 July 1925.

he would be given the job.[1] Shortly afterwards General Primo de Rivera gave a *fiesta andaluza* in honour of both the brothers, and his son José Antonio, a friend of the Machados, was prominent in organizing the national homage they earned with their play *La Lola se va a los puertos*.

The unfavourable reaction of the majority of Spanish intellectuals to Primo's dictatorship is generally known and has been described plainly enough by José Antonio: 'Dejaron solo al Dictador. Abrieron en torno suyo como un gran desierto. Quien osaba pisarlo renunciaba a toda esperanza de consideración entre los dispensadores de las jerarquías intelectuales.'[2] Although in an ambiguous position the Machados do not appear to have been ostracized in this fashion. Their relationship with the exiled Unamuno remained cordial and Ortega, also in Paris and bitterly critical of Primo, wrote personally to Manuel to congratulate him on his Directorship.[3] Certain of the younger writers were hostile to Manuel, it is true, but the five volumes of his *Obras completas* were well reviewed in the *Revista de Occidente*[4] and Jorge Guillén continued to welcome his collaboration in *Alfar*. And as Pedro Penzol remarked, Manuel's appearance in *Querschnitt* early in 1926, beside Lorca, Ortega, Unamuno and Picasso, indicated that he was far from discredited as an intellectual.[5] In fact outside

[1] Ricardo Fuente died 11 January 1925 (Cf. Machado's poem 'Semblanza de Ricardo Fuente'); within eight days Machado received the first request for an 'enchufe' from one Nicolás Salazar (letter Madrid, 19 January 1925, in the *BMB*).

[2] *Obras completas*, Ed. de F.E.T. de las J.O.N.S., Madrid, 1945, p. 696. The regime, as is known, was supported by few intellectuals besides Azorín, elected to the *Real Academia* in 1925, Maeztu, anxious to make the *Unión patriótica* intellectually respectable, and José María Pemán (first introduced to Machado by Enrique Paradas according to a letter from Cádiz, 9 January 1924, in the *BMB*).

[3] Letter, Paris, 20 July 1925, in the *BMB*.

[4] By Juan Chabás. Making the same point, J. F. Montesinos said of this article: 'Dieser Artikel ist interessant, weil in ihm einer der glänzendsten unter den jungen Dichtern Manuel Machado aufrichtige Bewunderung ausspricht, während seit dem Erscheinen von Manuel Machados letztem Buche unter den modernsten Schriftstellern eine gewisse Feindseligkeit gegen ihn herrscht' (*Die moderne spanische Dichtung*, p. 205). In fact, Machado was not publishing any new poetry of interest. His highly-paid contributions to *ABC* and *Blanco y Negro* were tired even if modern in the context of his work.

[5] In a letter, Leeds, 9 May 1926 (*BMB*).

Spain Machado's reputation was greater than ever during these years: in Europe and America Hispanists sang his praises and lectured on his work: Hans Juretschke in Frankfurt, Juan Chabás in Genoa, Pedro Penzol in Leeds, Fernando de Arteaga in Oxford, J. B. Trend in Cambridge, Douglas de Kalb in New York, Ernest Mérimée in Toulouse, W. C. Cooke in Cork, Jules Laborde, Carlos de Batlle and a host of others in Paris.

In Spain, Machado became still more famous as the co-author of a series of plays written in collaboration with Antonio, which were staged in close succession under the favourable conditions of the dictatorship.[1] Their names were well known to the theatre-going public long before the first of the series, *Desdichas de la fortuna*, opened in Madrid in February 1926. Manuel was of course famous as a theatre critic, and was powerfully connected with the Teatro español group through Ricardo Calvo and Jacinto Benavente, director there after 1919.[2] And in that theatre, in the early 'twenties, the brothers had already produced a series of translations and *refundiciones* of Spanish classics, subsidized by the Ayuntamiento of Madrid, and based on Manuel's research in the Biblioteca Municipal.[3] Impressed by the success of these versions of the

[1] These are listed in the bibliography. According to José Machado (*Últimas*, p. 90) and J. Sampelayo ('Una hora con Manuel Machado'), the collaboration between the two brothers was so close that it would be impossible to separate the individual contribution of either one of them. M. H. Guerra however attempts to do this in *El teatro de Manuel y Antonio Machado*.

[2] See Machado's article in *El Liberal*, 5 September 1919, and his reviews of Benavente's plays. A letter from Benavente, Madrid, 19 October 1925 (*BMB*) shows clearly enough his attitude to Machado: 'Agradecer una crítica laudatoria puede parecer solicitud de futuros elogios. Usted sabe que conmigo no hay ese compromiso. Usted es algo mejor que un buen crítico: un crítico bueno...todavía no ha llegado usted a la deshumanización del Arte. A esos que quieren el Arte tan puro que ni emocione ni interese, ni le importe a nadie.' R. Gullón's suggestion ('Relaciones...entre J.R.J. y M.M.') that the Machados were reacting against Benavente is unfortunate in view of the dedication of *Desdichas de la fortuna*, offered to Benavente in gratitude 'por el benévolo interés con que usted — el creador de todo un teatro — leyó esta humilde producción nuestra; por el generoso elogio que hizo usted de ella, antes de que fuese representada, y en testimonio de una admiración sin límites'.

[3] See José Machado, *Últimas*, p. 10, J. Díez-Canedo, '*Hernani* en Madrid', *El Sol* (Madrid), 2 January 1925 and J. M. de Sagarra's scornful comments on *El condenado por desconfiado* in *La Publicitat* (Barcelona), 3 January 1924.

Machados, Fernando Díaz de Mendoza and María Guerrero had encouraged them to write some original drama of their own, and it was the Díaz-Guerrero company which presented *Desdichas de la fortuna* in 1926. The play was a success,[1] and by the following September they had completed another one, *Juan de Mañara*, which was staged in the Teatro Reina Victoria in March 1927. Within the course of another year they wrote *Las adelfas* which was taken on tour in South America and the provinces before appearing in Madrid in October 1928. The leading role was taken by Lola Membrives who had also taken the lead in their version of *La niña de plata* in 1925. While admiring the Freudian psychoanalysis of *Las adelfas*, Lola Membrives's husband and manager Juan Reforzo anxiously reminded the Machados, late in 1927, of 'el compromiso de escribir, cuando puedan, un obra para Lola de verdadero caracter popular andaluz'.[2] *La Lola se va a los puertos*, written expressly for Lola Membrives, was produced in November 1929 in the theatre owned by the Marquis of Fontalba, a personal friend of Manuel's. Its success was enormous throughout Spain and South America. Offers were pressed on the Machados by a host of producers and the play was printed in over half a dozen editions. Juan Reforzo wrote that in Buenos Aires the Machados' fame eclipsed even that of Martínez Sierra, and in Barcelona María Palou lamented more bitterly than ever Manuel's preferring other actresses to her by entrusting them with his plays.[3]

[1] The performance coincided with the fiftieth anniversary of the *Institución libre*: in the course of an intimate gathering at Obelisco 14, M. B. Cossío praised the play for its theme of stoic honesty ('Homenaje'); see also José Machado, *Últimas*, p. 11 and a letter from M. B. Cossío, Madrid, 22 May 1926, in the *BMB*.

[2] From a letter, Buenos Aires, 13 November 1927 (*BMB*). Machado's friendship with Lola Membrives began with her letter from Santiago de Chile of 27 November 1920 thanking him for a kind report in *La Libertad*; see too the poem 'A Lola Membrives "creadora" de *La Lola*'. E. Gómez de Baquero wrote of her tremendous skill as a singer of Andalusian *coplas* in 'El *Ars moriendi* de Manuel Machado'.

[3] In two letters, Barcelona, 22 December 1929, and April 1931 (*BMB*); María Palou felt particularly cheated ('Ay, y a ver si hablamos también de ese arroz que por su mala memoria se quedó en el aire') because Machado had praised her so highly 'en aquellas décimas preciosas e inolvidables' in the poem 'Concepto, al estilo clásico'. Various attempts were made to film *La Lola* before J. de Orduña and J. Tordesilla's version appeared shortly after Manuel's death.

The Machados were fêted at the theatre and María Guerrero and Ricardo Calvo restaged *Desdichas de la fortuna* in their honour. At the height of their career as dramatists they were given a splendid banquet at the Ritz at which José Antonio Primo de Rivera made a laudatory speech.

In Antonio's lifetime only two more of the brothers' plays were produced: *La prima Fernanda* in April 1931 and *La duquesa de Benamejí* in March 1932. Under the changed conditions of the Second Republic they found it difficult to stage other plays they had written. In this connection the brothers' remarks on *La prima Fernanda*, a satire of the chaos and corruption of the latter days of the Dictatorship, are of the greatest interest. In *A.B.C.* they said they had intended the play to be staged before Primo's fall in January 1930 and therefore did not want it to be misunderstood as a 'superflua lanzada a moro muerto o burla, más o menos sarcástica, del caído'.[1] For this reason, however disillusioned they may have become with the Dictator, if not with his son, they were upset by the political capital that was made out of *La prima Fernanda* after the declaration of the Republic in April 1931.

In a series of press interviews the brothers pledged support to the Republic. In a joint interview with De Viu they approved outright of 'la derogación de la ley de Jurisdicciones, la del Código cavernario de Galo Ponte, la libertad de cultos, las reformas de Azaña en el Ejército, las que se proyectan e inician en Justicia,

---

[1] '*La prima Fernanda*', *A.B.C.*, 20(?) April 1931. It is curious that the brothers did not continue to stage their plays because they had one completed (*El hombre que murió en la guerra* — see A. de Obregón, *Arriba*, 19 April 1941 and Manuel's own 'Advertencia-Prólogo to the play, 18 April 1941), and at least three nearly completed (*La diosa Razón, El loco amor* and *Las brujas de Don Francisco* — see J. Sampelayo, 'M.M. en su jubilación'; M. J. Moya, 'Preguntas de *El Alcázar*' and D.F.B., 'Don Manuel Machado'). Pérez Ferrero says that *El hombre* was written for Ricardo Calvo (*Vida*, p. 168) but this seems unlikely since Antonio Machado confided to Juan Guerrero Ruiz in December 1935 that the play had not been staged 'por falta de un buen actor' (*Juan Ramón, de viva voz*, p. 445). Despite this, and despite his persistent lack of detail, Pérez Ferrero seemed to be hinting that the Machados' withdrawal from the theatre was connected with the change of regime in Spain: 'En 1931 cambia en muchas cosas la faz de España, debido a los acontecimientos políticos que traen la República, y, asimismo, cambia, en determinado sentido, la vida de estos dos poetas. Los asuntos teatrales adquieren otro ritmo' (*Vida*, p. 168).

Instrucción, Hacienda y Trabajo'.[1] But while Antonio preferred generally to keep his enthusiasm to himself, Manuel spread his abroad by composing a rousing new National Anthem, to the music of Oscar Esplá, which merited Juan Ramón Jiménez's disapproval.[2] But the Republic, so desired, soon ceased, in its turn, to be the darling of the brothers. The poem Manuel wrote, already in October 1932, for the *Asociación de escritores* on the death of Manuel de Sandoval, his exact contemporary, betrayed more than a lack of confidence in the new order:

> Hiciste bien, Manuel...Vino la hora
> de los muchos, funesta a los mejores;
> ....
>
> Adiós, contigo, al anhelar profundo
> de Belleza y Verdad...La sombra crece
> del milenario, que eludiste tú,
>
> abandonando, presuroso, un mundo,
> cuya suprema aspiración parece
> el plato de lentejas de Esaú.　　('A la oportuna muerte del
> 　　　　　　　　　　　　　poeta Manuel de Sandoval')

Throughout 1932 and 1933, frightened by the power of the mass parties in the Republican government, he unequivocally abandoned his Socialism and re-embraced his Liberalism, rejoicing in the return of the bullfighter El Gallo as the triumph of grace and splendour over the anonymous grey working mass of the people.[3] A definite turning point came in 1934. During this year of strikes and bloody repressions he lamented, in his regular column 'Antena' in *La Libertad*, the loss of individual personality to hostile mass groups. He reproached the students of Madrid University for demonstrating in sympathy with the workers in January 1934,

---

[1] 'Manuel y Antonio Machado disertan como convencidos republicanos'; this article, like one by Manuel Machado entitled 'La belleza de la República', is in a scrapbook in the *BMB*.

[2] J. Guerrero Ruiz, *Juan Ramón, de viva voz*, p. 158.

[3] 'El Gallo ha vuelto', *La Libertad*, 18 March 1934. See also *La Libertad*, 28 May 1933, when he boldly reaffirmed his Liberalism: 'Soy liberal en arte. Y romántico en política...Liberal y romántico, dos grandes palabras que hoy suenan casi totalmente a hueco. El mundo se debate hoy—lejos de toda libertad— entre dos dictaduras: la capitalista y la colectivista, la burguesa y la proletaria, entre el fascismo y el comunismo.—Ambas son para mí igualmente detestables'.

saying that in this way they managed only to 'engrasar inocente y absurdamente el caldo de los profesionales batallones de toda guerra civil'.[1] For political reasons he was forced to resign from *La Libertad* the following August. A note from the director, curt considering the history of Machado's collaboration with the paper, informed him that there was no longer any room for those 'fieles como usted aun a la orientación derechista que ha dejado de tener este diario'.[2]

As a result of this blow Machado withdrew to some extent from political and public life, content to seem an old Liberal horrified by the brutal innocence of a younger world. Now in his sixties, he relaxed to enjoy the quiet pleasures of a man past his prime but still warm with the glow of past glory. He avoided publicity and haunted the secluded areas of old Madrid. The cafés which he and Antonio (permanently in the capital after 1931) frequented were quiet and old fashioned: El Prado and El Español with their nine-teenth-century air, Las Delicias where they had a reserved table, and, to escape admirers, the Café de Valera with its blind pianist and its 'tertulias de mujeres románticas y cuarentonas'.[3] They shared their evenings in these cafés with José and old friends like Calvo and Ricardo Baroja as well as Zayas and Unamuno when they were in Madrid. A few others were also admitted to their confidence: J. M. de Cossío, M. Altolaguirre; and Pérez Ferrero, who used the occasion to gather material for his biography of the Machados. Although curiously unaware that Manuel had con-tinued to publish poetry in *La Libertad*, *A.B.C.* and *Blanco y Negro* continuously since *Ars moriendi*, Pérez Ferrero has given an inter-esting account of how M. Altolaguirre, during these gatherings, persuaded Manuel to publish another collection of verse in a luxurious edition supervised personally by Altolaguirre, with the appropriate and half-apologetic title of *Phoenix*.[4]

[1] 'La tragedia fea', *La Libertad*, 28 January 1934.
[2] From a letter, s.d. (1934), in the *BMB*. After its unequivocal beginnings, the political history of *La Libertad* was chequered.
[3] Pérez Ferrero, 'La última tertulia de los Machado'; see also I. Maffiotte, 'Hom-bres y cosas de Madrid'; R. Alberti, *Imagen*, p. 11; and a letter from A. Martínez (who admired the Machados from a distance at this time), Madrid, 21 April 1939, in the *BMB*.   [4] *Vida*, pp. 197–8.

José Machado's sentimental description of the last time Unamuno met the Machados in the café Varela, and how his image was reflected to infinity by the wall mirrors as he left the café, is in turn a fitting coda to the life Manuel and Antonio shared:

Recuerdo, últimamente, la tarde en que Unamuno, al despedirse del Poeta, le dijo: Hay una niebla tan espesa, que no se distingue nada.

Esto lo decía en vísperas de estallar la guerra. Después se alejó, cruzando rápido entre la doble hilera de espejos, que a un lado y a otro multiplicaban su figura en el larguísimo café de Varela. El Poeta lo siguió con los ojos hasta que desapareció por la puerta.

Fue ya ésta la última vez que se vieron.[1]

[1] *Últimas*, p. 24.

6

THE LEADEN RECONQUEST OF FAME
(1936–1947)

> Murió don Guido, un señor
> de mozo muy jaranero,
> muy galán y algo torero;
> de viejo, gran rezador.
> —Antonio Machado, 'Llanto de las virtudes
> y coplas por la muerte de don Guido'

The outbreak of the Civil War surprised Manuel Machado and his wife in Burgos where they were holidaying and visiting Eulalia's sister Carmen. The journey back to Madrid rapidly became impossible because, as one critic has put it, the capital was no longer part of Spain.[1] At first, unlike Unamuno cut off in Salamanca, Machado seems not to have realized the gravity of his situation. Unimpressed by the 'Cruzada', he expressed to a correspondent of the French periodical *Comédia* his annoyance at being inconvenienced by another Carlist war. This nonchalance provoked Mariano Daranás, a correspondent of *A.B.C.* who read Machado's remarks in Paris two months later, into a bitter attack on him, on this 'afortunado burócrata, colaborador y correligionario de Pedro Rico'[2] for his cynicism and earlier Socialist and Republican sympathies. An exchange of letters ensued in the columns of *El Castellano* of Burgos in which Machado vindicated himself agilely,

---

[1] M. Linares, 'Manuel Machado habla de su espíritu'. It is unlikely that Machado, forewarned of the rising, was escaping Madrid like those who flooded into Burgos at this time, frightened by the murder of Calvo Sotelo. Machado and his wife had been visiting Carmen on her Saint's day (16 July) for a number of years (see J. Arrarás, 'Fe y patriotismo'). A librarian in the Biblioteca Menéndez y Pelayo, Santander, told me that Machado had been visiting his 'hermanita Carmen' (as she is called in the dedication of *Sevilla y otros poemas*) at least since the 'twenties when she was in a convent in Santander before moving to Burgos.

[2] 'El comentario de un lírico burócrata', *A.B.C.*, 27 September 1936. Rico was a mayor of Madrid during the Republic.

insisting on his success under Primo de Rivera's regime rather than the Republic, and on his resignation from *La Libertad* for the right political reasons.[1] In fact by this time, September 1936, Daranás's watchdog concern for Machado's lack of team spirit was unnecessary. Finding himself obliged to live for an indefinite period in the clothes he stood in, in a city which offered him neither money nor means of earning any, and quickly sensitive to the fate of those uncommitted intellectuals who had not fled the country, he had already in August addressed himself to the Nationalist Propaganda Office in Burgos. In spite of bad health he worked hard enough to dissipate any doubts on anyone else's part and to become *bona fide* in the eyes of the propaganda chief Juan Pujol, through whose good offices he retrieved a post in the *Cuerpo facultativo*.

The poetry Machado wrote as propaganda, sonnets in praise of war heroes and the role of the New Spain in the world, bloomed with rare splendour in the cultural desert of the rebel zone and earned their author a peculiar desirability. The weekly *tertulia* at his flat, Calle Aparicio y Ruiz 8, attracted the aristocracy and military of Burgos and important Nationalist officials; he was overwhelmed by invitations to give recitals and talks, to publish newspaper articles and even comprehensive editions of his poetry in those difficult war-time conditions.[2] He was also asked to broadcast his work once the *Delegación del Estado para prensa y propaganda* had gained complete control of the *Radio nacional* in June 1937.[3] The climax of his reconquest of fame came early the following year when José María Pemán and Eugenio d'Ors told him that on the fifth of February he had been elected unanimously, if by the rump, to the Real Academia. He had just under a fortnight to prepare a speech before entering, on the nineteenth, 'el depósito

[1] See *El Castellano* (Burgos), 29 September, 6 and 7 October 1936.

[2] See F. Gallardo, 'El poeta Manuel Machado y su vida en Burgos'. The Falange printed most of Machado's earlier poetry as well as his propaganda in the three editions of *Poesía*. (*Opera omnia lyrica*); Ruiz Castillo, the editor of *Horas de oro*, said they were prepared to when he first suggested to Machado ('a salvo de la furia roja y en tierra de cristianos') that he could republish 'poesías ya recogidas en otros volúmenes' beside those 'inspirados en esta tragedia' and 'otros de espíritu religioso' (from a letter, Valladolid, 14 December 1937, in the *BMB*).

[3] See letters from Eugenio Vegas, Salamanca, 18 May and 31 May 1937, in the *BMB*.

de cosas eternas, honradas, cristianas y españolas'[1] then migrant at San Sebastián. He managed to compose a speech but added to his difficulties by choosing to talk about his life of all lives and in those circumstances. Although his poem to Franco was hailed as 'el primero de la España que nace',[2] and despite his discreet falsification of his own life story, the savage attack on French-inspired Romantic Liberalism which accompanied commentaries on his speech in the press, suggest that he had still misjudged the occasion.[3]

Were it not for the question of Machado's reawakened Christian faith, there would not be much point in discussing further his motives for supporting the rebellion of July 1936. When visiting his sister-in-law, the nun Carmen, in Burgos, one July before the Civil War, he made the acquaintance of the Jesuit José Zameza, the 'alumbrador de almas' to whom all the religious sonnets in *Horas de oro* were dedicated.[4] The priest gave him Saint

[1] As J. M. Pemán described it when he welcomed Machado into the Academy (*Unos versos*, p. 122); see also Pérez Ferrero, *Vida*, pp. 210–11.

[2] 'Los poetas', *La voz de España* (San Sebastián), 20 February 1938.

[3] By describing himself as 'el poeta menor, poeta del gesto inacabado' he provoked the reporter of *La voz de España* (20 February 1938) into exclaiming: 'De las dos literaturas, en tonos mayor y menor, preferimos para hoy, para estos momentos de guerra el Arte mayor, exaltado y grande de las grandes exclamaciones y narradas glorias'. And although he confused the dates of his works and protested he was free of French influence, the cry was still raised: 'Al eterno olvido las Mimís y las Margots y las orgías [all references to his poetry], los Verlaine, los Rimbaud, los Laforgue... ¡España! ¡Tradición, Dios, Caudillo, Imperio! ¡Versos, versos, versos! ¡Otra vez el alma hispana, en torrentes de emoción sincera, anegando los puntos de la pluma!' ('Manuel Machado ingresa en la Real Academia Española', *Unidad* (San Sebastián), 22 February 1938).

[4] Machado's copy of a book by Zameza, *Una Virgen apóstol* (Burgos, January 1935), in the *BMB*, has the inscription: 'A Manuel Machado, como recuerdo de un día feliz y santo' and another bears the words: 'A mi amadísimo y admirado amigo Manuel Machado, como recuerdo de ratos felices y santos' (*El alma de la iglesia misionera*, Burgos, September 1936). This suggests that Zameza, 'Profesor de misionología en la pontificia Universidad gregoriana de Roma', met Machado in the summer of 1935 and again the following year. The details Zameza remembered of his walks with Machado (in a letter from Rome, 5 January 1940, in the *BMB*), the medieval stone of Burgos and the chestnut trees beside the Arlanzón, certainly correspond to those in Machado's poem 'Burgos. Julio de 1935'.

Augustine's *Confessions*, offered to keep up a correspondence and encouraged him to go to Mass on the first Friday of the month. Later he wrote to Eulalia, whose faith had never faltered, advising her how best to carry on his work in his absence. And so, the son who had defied his father's anti-clericalism, the young man who was a furtive penitent in the Holy Week processions in Seville and who never quite forgot the Mary of Andalusian folklore, the man who even as the worldly journalist of *El Liberal* made pilgrimages to Santiago,[1] now, in middle-age, saw himself in Saint Augustine and in his whole life as a poet the yearning of a Verlaine or a Villon for heaven from the mud of the world. On entering Carmen's convent in July 1936, he claimed he had heard the voice of the Virgin Mary telling him to give himself to God and the New Spain: 'Debo a la Virgen del Carmen la fortuna de que todos esos acontecimientos me hayan sorprendido en Burgos.'[2] Friendships with the monks in the monastery of La Cartuja deepened; conversations with the Prior, don Agustín María Hospital, became more frequent and self-revelatory. In short Machado's growing spiritual dependency on a church whose politics, at least in that part of Spain, were hardly equivocal dissuaded him most effectively from, as Moreno Villa put it, vaulting over the frontier and landing by his brother's side.[3]

Manuel Machado vaulted over the frontier only at the end of the war: the story of his journey to Collioure to find both Antonio and his mother dead has been adequately told by others already.[4] From this distance their tragedy seems exemplary; in the hatred and the hysteria of the moment, Antonio no less than Manuel was forced to sacrifice personal sentiment to a devouring cause. Yet even at the height of the war Antonio appears to have tried to resolve this anomaly by evoking their common childhood.

[1] See *El Liberal*, 29 July 1918 and the poem 'Santiago de Compostela'. An unmistakably religious poem like 'La primera caída', first published in *Phoenix*, also shows that Machado's conversion was not entirely a product of the Civil War.
[2] See J. Arrarás, 'Fe y patriotismo'.
[3] Moreno Villa asked of Machado: ' ¿Cómo no diste un salto de garrocha y te plantaste con tu hermano más allá de la frontera?' ('La Manolería y el cambio').
[4] José Machado, *Últimas*, pp. 91 ff.; M. Pérez Ferrero, *Vida*, pp. 203 ff.; A. de Albornoz, *Poesías de guerra de A. Machado* (Puerto Rico, 1961).

Mi Sevilla infantil ¡tan sevillana!
¡cual muerde el tiempo tu memoria en vano!
¡Tan nuestra! Aviva tu recuerdo, hermano.
No sabemos de quién va a ser mañana.[1]

And on the other side Manuel's friend Dionisio Ridruejo has described the efforts of the Nationalist propagandists in Burgos to see Antonio still as Manuel's brother.[2] How much Manuel's pain was eased by the further well-intentioned but fantastic demonstrations of Antonio's secret allegiance to the 'Cruzada', which certain journalists saw fit to publish and even to send to Manuel personally on his return to Spain, is not easy to assess, despite his claim that they were like sunshine in moments of despair.[3]

Once Franco had taken the capital Manuel Machado left Burgos with his wife to welcome him there, asking God in the poem 'Saludo a Franco' to bless the holy enterprise that had unsheathed his sword and given him victory. He found his flat in Churruca unstricken by the Asiatic plague he had so uncharitably cursed and unscathed by the rain of Nationalist shells of the previous three years. Murillo's Virgins, dusted, gazed as serenely as ever from the walls; for the last few cold days of March the finely carved *camilla* was brought out and with time the scent of fresh spikenards pervaded the rooms as before.[4] After the formality of a secret police vetting he retrieved his former post as Director of the Museo municipal and of Investigaciones históricas del Ayuntamiento, discreetly using his influence to prevent the dismissal of subordinates with dubious political backgrounds. He frequented the cafés Lyon and La Criolla with old friends, Ricardo Calvo, Gerardo Diego, Antonio de Zayas, Rincón Lazcano and Antonio Casero; again the rhythm of the days became regular and everything seemed to be not very different from what it had been before the war.

But what change!

In the prologue he wrote in Paris at the end of the war for

---

[1] *Hora de España* (Valencia), 18, pp. 8–9.
[2] 'El poeta rescatado', *Escorial* (Madrid), November 1940, p. 99.
[3] See M. de la Concepción Pérez Zalabardo, 'Sobre la muerte y la vida de Antonio Machado'.
[4] J. M. de Cossío, 'Recuerdo de Manuel Machado', J. Sampelayo, 'Una hora con Manuel Machado' and J. López Ruiz, 'Entierro de los restos mortales'.

Pérez Ferrero's biography of the Machados, Gregorio Marañón described the brothers as two supreme representatives of a vanished Golden Age. Indeed Manuel was the survivor not just of his family; his former acquaintances formed a world which had ceased to exist. For as well as Antonio, Ramiro de Maeztu, Francisco Villaespesa, Ramón del Valle-Inclán and Miguel de Unamuno, all intimates of his youth, had also died during the war or just before it; Juan Ramón Jiménez, José Moreno Villa and Juan Chabás had disappeared from Spain and from his life; Jorge Guillén and Ramón Gómez de la Serna, though they wrote to Machado from abroad, were ghosts in Madrid; Jacinto Benavente and Pío Baroja were still in exile and Antonio Lezama, trapped in the Chilean Embassy, communicated only to beg Machado, for the sake of their old friendship, to do all he could to save Miguel Hernández's life.[1] Outwardly Machado, with his enigmatic smile and confident bearing, showed himself unaffected by this huge bereavement; but those who knew him well have hinted at secret depressions which towards the end of his life developed into a morbid pessimism. The uneasiness of the marriage between what was left of a vanished era and the beginnings of a new one was obvious in the preface to *Poesía. Opera omnia lyrica*, a series of eulogies of Manuel Machado by 'varios ingenios': José María Pemán, Antonio de Zayas, Gerardo Diego, Luis Rosales, Leopoldo Panero, Dionisio Ridruejo, Luis Felipe Vivanco, Alfonso Moreno and others.

Two months after the end of the war, Pedro de Répide wrote to Manuel Machado that he was looking forward to taking a leading role with him in the cultural activities in Madrid on his return to Spain, and added: 'Ahora ya se podrá hacer todo sin la roña socialista'.[2] He was not disappointed. Machado was prominent in directing culture in post-war Spain in various ways; as a judge of national literary competitions on repeated occasions, as a founder member of the group *Musa musae*, or more curiously as 'camarada Machado' of the *Consejo asesor de Cultura de la O.J.* Even in this pre-eminent position he ran into trouble with the censor; gener-

---

[1] In a letter from the Embajada de Chile, 25 January 1940, in the *BMB*.
[2] In a letter from Caracas, 10 May 1939, in the *BMB*.

ally however he fulfilled quite adequately the part assigned him by the *Subsecretaría de prensa y propaganda* and other controlling bodies.[1] His poetry, both religious and patriotic, became staple fare in schools and was set to music and performed publicly; for a procession to the Pilar in Zaragoza, for instance, he composed three 'letrillas piadosas, patrióticas y llenas de sentido'[2] to be sung to the tune of the National Anthem. This was in September 1939 and the following year, to celebrate the nineteenth centenary of the Virgin's appearance in that city in mortal flesh, he wrote *El Pilar de la Victoria*, a play designed to excite love as much for Franco's regime as for God, with its scenes of Catalans and Basques, Galicians and Valencians dancing in amicable unity before 'la Patrona de España'.[3]

When they were both young men, Juan Ramón Jiménez had said of Manuel Machado: 'Acabará por andar, como Enrique Heine, ocho años en su lecho, con los párpados caídos y las manos sin carne. Tendrá también que apuntalar su divinidad en cualquier establecimiento balneario.'[4] Jiménez's prophesy proved to be too pessimistic, for although Machado suffered increasingly from bronchitis his bearing remained imposing and he vigorous enough to continue to flatter actresses and adolescent girls with his habitual gallantry.[5] Moreover, as we have seen, in the immediate post-war years, others, not he, firmly and effectively shored up his divinity. But towards the very end of his life this support fell away, noticeably so after his forced retirement from the Museo Municipal in August 1944. In fact his retiring generally from prominence, from

[1] At their behest he contributed to *Occident* (Paris) from January 1940 onwards, and to the cultural exchange with Italy the same year.

[2] As Fray Bruno de San José described them in a letter from Madrid, 7 June 1939 (*BMB*).

[3] Machado believed the play to be the one he had written 'con mayor fervor y emoción' (J. Sampelayo, 'Una hora con M.M.'). Before his death Pablo Luna began work on a musical accompaniment for the play and Julio Gómez completed the score (A. Araiz, 'Anoche se leyó *El Pilar*..., la obra póstuma del maestro Luna', *Amanecer* (Zaragoza), 27 September 1944). Luna's widow helped to finance a performance of the musical version in the Teatro principal, Zaragoza (see *El Noticiero* and *Amanecer*, both local newspapers, 13 October 1944).

[4] *La corriente*, p. 43.

[5] See the dedications in *Cadencias de cadencias*; J. Sampelayo, 'Manuel Machado en su jubilación' and R. Gullón, *Conversaciones*, p. 42.

about this time on, was symptomatic of important changes in Spain. A growing sophistication in the world of letters and the fact that *Garcilaso* and *Escorial*, which Machado had supported, were no longer the sole reviews of consequence, meant that his post-war work, once praised as the epic of the New Spain and so on, was now, like its author, quietly put on one side and, with a knowing look, forgotten. The guarded homages paid to Antonio on the anniversaries of his death, to which Manuel assiduously contributed, nevertheless showed him clearly, as the praise of the dead poet grew less and less apologetic, how much the cult of the one brother was waxing as that of the other waned.[1] In some circles he was openly scorned and he withdrew into the more hospitable world of old school comradeship.[2]

In these last years of his life the Jesuit Father Cavestany assumed Father Zameza's role of Machado's spiritual mentor. The beads of his rosary, the gift of the Prior of La Cartuja, passed through his fingers with the ease of old habit, and he said that had it not been for his wife he would gladly have renounced the bestiality of the world, as absolutely as Einar, and entered a monastery himself.[3] The themes of his last poems were exclusively religious, even mystical; and, ironically, the same spirit which had originally made it easier for him to accept Franco's regime now led him to criticise it, guardedly, in newspaper articles which gained him the shy adhesion of his readers.[4]

[1] With Manuel's help, J. Ortiz de Pinedo produced a wireless programme, in commemoration of Antonio's death, in 1943, and the following year Manuel and Dionisio Ridruejo (famous for his outspoken edition of Antonio's poems in 1941) organized a 'homenaje' (see letters, from Zaragoza, 5 February 1943, and from Madrid, 2 February 1944, respectively, in the *BMB*).

[2] He was viciously attacked, for example, by P. Álvarez Fernández in *La estafeta literaria*, no. 8 (1944). He suffered in any case as a result of the general change in literary taste marked by the appearance of *Espadaña* in 1944, but J. R. Jiménez was of the opinion that in the end he was 'despreciado hasta por los franquistas' (*El modernismo*, p. 189). For his association with 'Los del '90', fellow old boys of Cardenal Cisneros, see J. Álvarez-Sierra, *A.B.C.*, 18 November 1956 and F. Allué y Morer, 'Un hermano de los Machado'.

[3] See L. de Armiñán, 'M.M. ha muerto' and P. Cantu, 'M.M. ha dejado escritas sus memorias'.

[4] 'El quinto no matar', 'Aquí, al que manda' and 'Ejercicios de sentido común', *A.B.C.*, 8 April, 23 May and 11 November 1946 respectively; his readers' letters are in the *BMB*.

On returning home from the funeral of a friend one bitter January day in 1947 he felt ill enough to take to his bed. In just under a fortnight, on the nineteenth, he died of bronchial pneumonia. For his burial the following afternoon, the bells tolled as they did for Don Guido. Behind his coffin, where he lay dressed in a Franciscan habit, his arms crossed on his chest, walked Eugenio d'Ors, José María Pemán, Luca de Tena and Serrano Suñer; Azorín, Benavente, Sassone and Gerardo Diego; Vivanco, Rosales and Panero; his brother Francisco. The Real Academia ordered fifty masses to be said for his soul.[1]

Homages there were few. As a journalist remarked, like that of Manuel de Sandoval, his death was timely and opportune.[2]

His goods were left to the Church; his library, which included books of Antonio's, to the Institución Fernán-González in Burgos.

Eulalia entered a convent in Barcelona, where she still lives.

[1] See a letter from J. Casares to Machado's widow, Madrid, 24 January 1947 (*BMB*); J. López Ruiz, 'Entierro de los restos mortales'; and Fray Esteban Ibáñez O.B.M., 'Seis figuras famosas del arte y de las letras españolas mueren con el hábito franciscano', *Signo* (Madrid), 1 February 1947.

[2] J. Ramón Aparicio, 'A un raro', *Amanecer*, 28 January 1947, referring in turn to Machado's poem 'A la oportuna muerte de...M. de Sandoval'. The press in general was prolific but perfunctory; some of the articles by Machado's friends Gerardo Diego, Azorín, E. d'Ors, E. Carrère, J. M. Pemán, L. J. Vivanco and P. de Répide (all listed in the Bibliography) are of interest, and the tributes by J. García Nieto and R. Montesinos (*El Español*, 25 January 1947) were more than courteous. But L. Rodríguez Alcalde was still almost alone in trying honestly to revindicate Machado in 'Elegía y reivindicación de don Manuel Machado', *Alerta* (Santander), 22 January 1947. The only other obituary of critical interest was Dámaso Alonso's 'Ligereza y gravedad'.

7

MODERNISM

Románticos somos... ¿Quién que Es no es romántico?
—Rubén Darío, 'La canción de los pinos'

Manuel Machado's writing, more specifically his poetry, is best understood as the product of a Modernist; and if the idea of his being a Modernist is difficult, the difficulty is not to show that he was one. Critics, whether deploring or praising it, have been unanimous in emphasizing the large Modernist element in his poetry. Some went so far as to hail him as the unrivalled master of the movement.[1] For one he was 'uno de sus mejores sacerdotes, acaso el más iniciado';[2] for another he began and ended the whole Modernist era in Spain;[3] a third repeated: 'De hecho sería él, mejor que ningún otro de los poetas españoles, quien representaría en toda su amplitud el movimiento.'[4] Nor was Machado silent on the subject himself. *Electra, La revista ibérica* and *Juventud* were the weapons he and fellow Modernists used to attack the uncomprehending public and the hostile critic; his article 'El modernismo y la ropa vieja', in *Juventud,* was one of the most passionate written in defence of the movement. And did he not choose *La Guerra Literaria* as a title, and style himself a soldier in his personal account of the origins, aims and development of Modernism in Spain? Clearly, the problem is not whether he was a Modernist or not, but what being a Modernist meant.

As a term of abuse hurled at Machado and his contemporaries, the word had force but little precision. In the streets of Madrid at the turn of the century, the insult 'Modernist', 'la palabreja' as Machado called it,[5] was directed indiscriminately at those whose behaviour and dress—and only incidentally whose poetry—

[1] For example, Gerardo Diego in 'Poetas del '98'.
[2] C. Santos González, in his prologue to the second edition of *Alma.*
[3] M. Mantero, 'Los toros'.   [4] F. de Onís, *Antología,* p. 245.
[5] See p. 20 above.

offended against the standards of the society of the time. The word attracted the emotional discharges of Grand Old Men, notably Ferrari and Echegaray, and became 'un dicterio complejo de toda clase de desprecios',[1] a curse for general usage which served as a scapegoat for the most catholic of guilts and exasperations. How else could one understand for instance the overtly 'moral' invective of Father Juan Mir?: 'La corrupción del deslavado Modernismo llega hasta las entrañas mismas de la lengua, cuya gramática trastorna, cuyas leyes deja burladas, cuyos modismos adultera, cuyas frases suple con otras desatinadas, impropias del castizo romance.'[2] It is clear that being a Modernist was a bad and outlandish thing; it is not clear what scope the term should have in literary criticism.

Definitions of the Modernist movement by its historians have been either boldly comprehensive or timidly narrow. On the one hand it has been stretched to the proportions of a universal crisis in human civilization. On the other it has been restricted to the idiosyncrasies of this or that literary clique in Spain or Spanish America early this century. It was Federico de Onís who first put forward the crisis theory, in a much quoted passage of 1934:

El Modernismo es la forma hispánica de la crisis universal de las letras y del espíritu que inicia hacia 1895 la disolución del siglo XIX y que se había de manifestar en el arte, la ciencia, la religión, la política y gradualmente en los demás aspectos de la vida entera, con todos los caracteres, por lo tanto, de un hondo cambio histórico cuyo proceso continúa hoy.

The only characteristic the Modernists had in common, he argued, was their desire, in D'Annunzio's words, to 'rinnovarsi o morire', according to the dictates of their own extreme subjectivism; or, in other words, that they had nothing tangible in common at all, and that a school of Modernism would be the negation of its essence.[3] Following Onís, Juan Ramón Jiménez, among many others, was capable of reaching out just as bravely into abstraction when thinking of Modernism, thereby invalidating the force of the

---

[1] *La Guerra Literaria*, p. 25.
[2] In an essay of 1908, quoted by M. Henríquez Ureña, *Breve historia*, p. 165.
[3] *Antología*, pp. xiv–xv. Critics of Modernism have been usefully divided into categories by N. J. Davison, *The Concept of Modernism in Hispanic Criticism*, Boulder, Colorado, 1966.

ideas he derived directly from his personal experience. He claimed that Modernism was not just a Hispanic affair but a European epoch, no less portentous than the Renaissance itself: he adduced as evidence the phenomena both of a reformist movement within the Roman Catholic Church condemned by Pius X in 1907, incidentally called Modernism, and of Santiago Rusiñol's *Festes Modernistes*, at first an independent movement in Catalonia concerned mainly with the visual arts and the theatre.[1] Arqueles Vela, in his *Teoría literaria del modernismo* (Mexico, 1949), went even further, attaining sheer geometric perfection with his notion of Modernism as the confluence of the modern spirit of the ancient world with the ancient spirit of the modern world. By contrast, others have reduced the orbit of Modernism with fastidious meanness: notably those writers actually involved in the movement. Darío used the word differently from Villaespesa, who used it differently from Rodó. Discriminations of this kind have persisted. Debates still continue about whether Julián del Casal, Manuel José Othón and José Martí can be considered Modernists or not. And in Spain, Guillermo Díaz-Plaja set a fashion of limiting Modernism in yet another way by making it the effeminate opposite of the virile reforming movement of the 'noventa y ochistas' in his book *Modernismo frente al noventa y ocho*.

At this stage, then, it becomes necessary to do what Max Henríquez Ureña began to do in his *Breve Historia del Modernismo*: to restate plain things plainly.[2] First: Modernism was a literary movement in the Spanish language, principally involving writers of poetry and fiction. It may be stimulating and even instructive to draw parallels between Modernist literature and certain con-

---

[1] J. R. Jiménez, quoted by G. Díaz-Plaja, *Poesía lírica española* (Barcelona, 1937), p. 351. For Catalan Modernism, see J. F. Ráfols, *Modernismo y modernistas* (Barcelona, 1949) and A. Cirici Pellicer, *El arte modernista* (Barcelona, 1951); and note 2 on p. 99 below. More recently, R. Gullón, *Direcciones del Modernismo*, and I. A. Schulman, 'Reflexiones en torno a la definición del Modernismo' (*Cuadernos Americanos*, CXLVII (July–August 1966), pp. 211–40), have used Jiménez's ideas as a necessary antidote to the narrowness of critics like Raúl Silva Castro who restrict the idea of Modernism to the bounds of Darío's writings.

[2] The approach to Modernism adopted here has also been suggested by A. Valbuena Prat, *La poesía española contemporánea* (Madrid, 1930).

temporary trends in music, theology or painting; but not at the expense of ignoring or underestimating the real and peculiar complexities of the literary medium. Secondly: almost without exception the writers involved in the movement were aware of each other's existence and conscious of a common affiliation, whether they were active in Havana, Mexico, Lima, Santiago, Buenos Aires, Montevideo or Madrid. The period of their spiritual association can be charted historically by means of the dates of the periodicals they founded and distributed and of their books: *Azul...* (1888), *Nieve* (1893), *Prosas profanas* (1896), *Las montañas del oro* (1897), *Ritos* (1898), *Castalia bárbara* (1899), *La copa del rey de Thule* (1900), *Ninfeas* (1900), *Los arrecifes de coral* (1901), *Lascas* (1901), *Minúsculas* (1901), *Rimas de sombra* (1902), *El alto de los bohemios* (1902), *Poemas rústicos* (1902), *Alma* (1902), *Soledades* (1902), *La paz del sendero* (1903), *Cantos de vida y esperanza* (1905), *Caprichos* (1905). Thirdly: all the Modernist writers were strongly influenced by French Romantic and post-Romantic writers, notably by the Parnassians. The actual process of absorption of ideas and techniques from France was admittedly long and intricate; and it is true, as in the case of José Asunción Silva, for instance, that France was not always the only source. But still there can be no doubt about the main importance of Parnassianism. Darío, the originator of the movement, and Manuel Machado, its most representative exponent in Spain, are both good test-cases. Both poets follow the Parnassians in a sophisticated irruption into the exotic and the exquisite, the primitive and the archaic; an irruption which with time stocked the *musée imaginaire* of the modern world and Machado's own 'Museo'.

In Spanish America the Modernists explored, superficially, the strange indigenous cultures of their continent; although, like their Romantic predecessors, they extracted little human substance, for the same reason as they turned just as readily to the Far East and Japan with its kimonos and geisha girls. Machado's Parnassian curiosity was more limited and did not go beyond Cleopatra's Egypt ('Oriente'), Renaissance Italy ('Oliveretto de Fermo'), the fairy-tale lands of Wagner ('Wagner') and the deserts of the Near East ('Oasis'); and of course medieval Spain. The interest shown generally at this period by Spanish writers in their national origins stemmed not just from a desire for regeneration and a repugnance towards the Spain of the Hapsburgs and the Counter-Reformation; it was also stimulated by the aesthetic attitude which found the exotic and the archaic similarly fascinating.[1] This is very clear in Darío's (French-inspired) 'Cosas del Cid' and Machado's 'Don Carnaval', 'Alvar-Fáñez', 'Glosa', and above all in his 'Castilla', whose origins are very un-Castilian. The same is true of the Spanish Modernists' taste for primitive, popular or folk poetry in Spanish, the ambiguity of their attitude being more than easily accommodated in that most treacherous of adjectives, 'popular'.

In all this, in their exoticism, their archaism and their primitivism, the Modernists were drawing heavily on Parnassian precedent. It is, however, often difficult to distinguish what in their work derived from Leconte de Lisle, Hérédia and Théophile Gautier, and what from Hugo and the Romantics. This is not surprising or discouraging, since the distinction between the two movements is often hard to make even within the limits of the French poetic tradition; and it is positively helpful in so far as it reminds us of the basic connection between Modernism and Romanticism. The Modernists' impatience with Renaissance and neoclassical literary theory was the same as that shown by the Romantics. Their refusal to defer to authority in rhetoric and poetics was similarly inspired and similarly expressed; so was their search for cultures alien to the Western classical tradition and their corresponding revaluation of that tradition. For Darío, as for his French predecessors, 'las mágicas fragancias que hicieran los delirios de las liras' in Greece and Rome ('Divagación') were no more and no less authoritative and indicative than 'el sonoro chino' or the bewitching song of the Lorelei. And in hailing poets as celestial lightning conductors ('¡Torres de Dios!'), transmitters of divine inspiration and not the pale reflectors of circumstance, he was saying what Hugo and others had said fifty years before him.[2] The Modernists' impatience, as Romantics, with neoclassicism even outweighed their fascination, as Parnassians, for the exqui-

---

[1] See Manuel Machado, 'El '98 y yo', *Arriba*, 12 December 1946.
[2] See M. H. Abrams, *The Mirror and the Lamp* (O.U.P., 1953).

site. This is plain in Manuel Machado's response to eighteenth-century France, which rarely transcends caricature. Florian may have been the 'rimador de una Arcadia elegantísima, correcta...', but he beat his mistresses unmercifully. The charm of Florian's culture was precisely that of one that was gone for good:

> siglo de encajes y rimas,
> minuetos, clavicordios...
> galante, enciclopedista,
> que pintó las miniaturas
> e inventó la guillotina, ('Fin de siglo')[1]

There is little justification for describing Modernism as a reaction against Romanticism and the nineteenth-century literary tradition as long as the word Romanticism retains the meaning it normally has in a European context. Those critics who, rightly, insist on the Modernists' rejection of poets like José Zorrilla and Esteban Echeverría are wrong when they attribute this rejection to these poets' Romanticism and not to their rhetorical excesses: to their lack of Romantic sensibility, in fact. Realizing this, Manuel Machado found it necessary to show himself indebted, as a Modernist, to 'los matices de la poesía nueva'[2] in Zorrilla's poetry and to emphasize that little-appreciated aspect of the Spanish Romantic:

> Decid que fue también aura y vislumbre,
> temblor de luna en misterioso lago,
> secreto dulce, tierna mansedumbre,
> fino matiz, presentimiento vago. ('A Zorrilla')

As for Bécquer, a far less equivocal Romantic and closer to, say Wordsworth or Eichendorff, the Modernists respected him with-

---

[1] Cf. too 'Siglo XVIII'. Machado takes the princess in 'Figulinas' more seriously, it is true, admiring the way her exquisite elegance hides the fact of her animality and that she must, like him, suffer and die. But he still recognized that the classical ideal was no longer viable for him, even when admitting that: 'Mi gusto sería vivir y escribir las serenidades bucólicas de Virgilio o—más abajo—los elegantes y fríos madrigales de los clásicos del siglo de oro, paisanos míos. Esa escuela sevillana, tan fina y tan fría. O, en todo caso, ser un Horacio a lo Fray Luis.' In fact he saw himself as a companion of the Romantics, of Poe, Heine, Verlaine and Bécquer, 'aventureros del ideal a través de las pasiones amargas y de la vida rota' (*La Guerra Literaria*, pp. 117–18).

[2] *La Guerra Literaria*, p. 21; see also his remarks on Espronceda, p. 45.

out exception.[1] Modernism seemed modern in the Spanish-speaking world largely because of the small impact that Romanticism made on the Spanish literary tradition. The ease with which the Romantics were eclipsed in Spain by the so-called Eclectics is proof of this weakness. And in Spanish America, the cradle of Modernism, its measure is the fact that the reputation of traditionalists like Olmedo and Bello, questioned in the middle of the century, actually increased in what has been described as the neoclassical convalescence of the 1860s and 1870s. Indeed, when he first used the term 'Modernism' in a consciously specific way in 1888, Darío defined it as a resistance to the 'tomados moldes de hierro'[2] which were still then cramping poetry in Spanish.

This backwardness cannot be dissociated from the social and intellectual history of Spain and Spanish America in the nineteenth century. E. Allison Peers, urging the importance of Spanish Romanticism, rarely associates the movement with this background. Indeed, he has no alternative, in contrast to the polemical Menéndez y Pelayo who, arguing the opposite case far more persuasively, scrupulously attributes the few hints of Romantic revolution visible in Spanish literature to an accidental infringement of an otherwise well-maintained orthodoxy. In poetics, this orthodoxy depended on the observance of rules established in Europe during the Renaissance, which were subsequently glossed and variously interpreted, but whose ultimate validity was the authority of quotations from works by Greek and Roman theorists. Like the authorities in astronomy and anatomy before them, these classical literary preceptors were discredited as such towards the end of the eighteenth century, ultimately as a consequence of the growing status of empirical science and of a new inquiring independence. During the first half of the nineteenth century, a period of great development in Europe, Spain had no scientists, and no intrepid iconoclasts: the Spanish Romantics' desire to divest themselves

---

[1] His influence on Manuel Machado is incontestable in poems like 'Melancolía' and 'Eleusis'. For this and other reasons J. L. Cano's argument in De Machado a Bousoño (Madrid, 1955) is tendentious: he argues that Manuel Machado was the more a Modernist for being concerned with 'la belleza exterior' of poetry and unsusceptible to Bécquer's influence.

[2] In an essay quoted by M. Henríquez Ureña, Breve historia del Modernismo, p. 157.

of authority found little support in the intellectual climate of their society.

In so far as Romanticism was more than a formal rebellion, the relationship between the history of ideas and poetic practice is more problematic. Few Romantics were as explicit and as comprehensive as Wordsworth was when he accommodated the new sources of his (Romantic) inspiration in a creed which was a whole attitude to life and an explanation of the universe in open contrast to the mechanical explanation offered by the empirical scientists of his time. But many echoed his response, if less amply, to what became an increasingly oppressive constant of nineteenth-century history: the scientists' account of man's place in the universe and his origins. The absence, or suppression, of that uncomfortable philosophy in Spain is obvious from the preoccupations of her Romantic writers, which were marginal to it, and from the tone, for example, of Valera's review of *Azul...* as late as 1888. For Valera complains almost flippantly of Darío's foreign modernity and of his familiarity with the philosophy in which: 'El conjunto de los seres, el Universo, todo cuanto alcanzan a percibir la vista y el oído, ha sido, como idea, coordinado metódicamente en una anaquelería o casillero para que se comprenda mejor.' This did not prevent him from identifying the Romantic nature of Darío's response to this philosophy: 'Que en este infinito tenebroso e incognoscible perciba la imaginación, así como en el éter, nebulosas o semilleros de astros, fragmentos y escombros de religiones muertas, con los cuales procura formar algo nuevo como ensayo de nuevas creencias y de renovadas mitologías.'

In these broader terms Manuel Machado justifies supremely both his office as the high-priest of Spanish Modernism, and the connection between Modernism and Romanticism.[1] In his case

[1] Cf. C. G. Amézaga, who said of his Modernist contemporaries: '*Romanticismo puro*,—dirá quizá, displicente, alguien que no cree ya compatibles con nuestro modo de ser, las manifestaciones artísticas de esa escuela. ¡Y qué engañados los que se figuran tal cosa! El romanticismo vive en la especie humana como una de esas tendencias incorregibles de su propia naturaleza. El creciente desarrollo de las ideas materialistas, sus enemigas, no llega a minorar en el hombre la fantasía, base de toda creación romántica en el consorcio del sentimiento' ('Manuel Gutiérrez Nájera', *Poetas mexicanos*, Buenos Aires, 1896, pp. 275–94. Reprinted in *Manuel Gutiérrez Nájera. Florilegio crítico-conmemorativo*, Mexico, Ediciones de Andrea,

the provocation, like the response, was unusual. For his father, Antonio Machado y Álvarez, was one of the few intellectuals in nineteenth-century Spain to keep abreast of scientific developments abroad and to urge the consequences of these developments on to Spanish society in an aggressive way. His Sevillian group was the first to translate Spencer's books into Spanish, and he himself, alone among his contemporaries, ended up adopting the extreme position of an Haeckelian, channelling his impatience with Spanish backwardness into an uncompromising scientific determinism. Manuel absorbed the facts his father retailed, witnessing his demonstrations of the undivine origins of man and his anthropological explorations into myth and society.[1] But the instruction prompted him not to contribute further to the scientific explanation of man, but to synthesize, in the poem 'Eleusis', the emotional consequences of what he had learnt already.

Eleusis, not Athens. Machado's soul on its restless pilgrimage goes back in time through the forests of the German iron age:

> Se fue hasta el castillo
> del burgrave fiero
> que está en la alta roca;
> los puentes cayeron
> y se despertaron
> los sones de hierro.

Still mesmerized by the glimpse of Ceres, the earth-goddess, he crosses over the green Ionian plains without peace or pause, dragged on by a treacherous undertow which upsets the classical stasis:

> Se fue hasta las verdes
> llanuras de Jonia; y el templo
> cruzó de Partenes.
> Del mármol eterno
> dejó las regiones...

1966). Manuel Machado also referred to this 'growing development' when in *La Guerra Literaria*, he spoke of society in late nineteenth-century Spain as 'despreciando las letras y las artes en gracia al amor de las ciencias entonces victoriosas en el mundo..., despreciando cuanto se ignoraba' (p. 19). The case for the strong connection between Romanticism and Modernism has again been argued recently by D. L. Shaw, '*Modernismo*: A contribution to the Debate', *Bulletin of Hispanic Studies*, XLIV (1967), pp. 195–202.

[1] See my article 'Antonio Machado y Álvarez and Positivism'.

Then on back again, past Celtic gold, black stones and 'fragmentos y escombros de religiones muertas':

> Oro y negras piedras,
> y muros inmensos,
> y tumbas enormes
> —sepulcro de un pueblo
> que mira hacia Oriente
> con sus ojos muertos—

Then back further still, to the most primitive of civilizations and the pre-rational source of life and culture in the dark forests of a dream. In its cultural catholicity Machado's pilgrimage is like Darío's in 'Divagación'. But 'Eleusis' as a poem is austerer and more closely worked; it has a temporal as well as a spatial dimension, and exposes the more rigorously the common root of fascination for the archaic and the exotic. In short it is the best indication and the most accomplished expression by a Spanish Modernist of the cultural significance of that movement.

8

A FORMAL REVOLUTION

A satisfying way of demonstrating the impact of Modernism on poetry in Spanish, and on Machado's poetry in particular, is to describe the revolution it caused in the use of verse form, metre and rhyme, a revolution begun only half-heartedly by the Spanish Romantics. The progress of the movement, and of a poet like Machado within it, can be measured in detail in the growing emancipation from the limited number of verse-forms which were considered obligatory until the end of the nineteenth century. It is true that many of the Modernists' formal innovations and iconoclastic experiments were simply exercises for their own sake. Salvador Rueda, embittered by jealousy of Darío, significantly based his claim to having been the true founder of Modernism on the number of new metres and rhythms he had invented and introduced into Spanish poetry. As a result, there has been a tendency among critics to think of the Modernist movement as primarily a technique, a tendency which affected Dámaso Alonso in his essay on Manuel Machado: 'Modernismo es, ante todo, una técnica; la posición del 98—digámoslo en alemán para más claridad—una *Weltanschauung*. Aquí descansa la diferenciación esencial. Quiere esto decir que 'modernismo" y "actitud del 98" son conceptos incomparables, no pueden entrar dentro de una misma línea de clasificación, no se excluyen mutuamente.'[1] The Modernists were admittedly obsessed with form and its refinements: but this does not authorize us to separate, pedagogically, simplistically, 'form' from 'content', and it does not excuse the failure to realize that the Modernists' rearticulation of the Spanish poetic language was in the first place the physical expression of a new sensitivity, of a new *Weltanschauung*.

With the exception of two poems, '. . . ?' (*sic*) and 'Mis amores',

[1] 'Ligereza y gravedad', p. 91.

both *seguidillas* in *Tristes y Alegres*, all the verse which Manuel Machado published before the group of poems which appeared in *Electra* fits perfectly within the limits of traditional forms. No less than 40% of the poems in *Tristes y Alegres* are *silvas* of 7 and 11 syllables with impeccable rhyme schemes, and 20% are regularly accented 11-syllable quatrains. Even the sonnets, 'Ella' and 'Lo que dicen las cosas', which appeared in the Modernist-directed *Madrid Cómico* and *La vida literaria* as late as December 1898 and March 1899 respectively, like all the others of the pre-Paris period, were classical in number of syllables, rhyme and caesura. It must be concluded that the alexandrine sonnet Machado had to justify before the academic Benot as a separate type, a 'sonite', was written not, as Machado suggested, before, but after, his first journey to France.[1]

Machado rarely created new verse-forms for their own sake; Unamuno observed quite justly that 'Machado no es ningún virtuoso de la versificación, sino un poeta'. Rather than invent, for the most part he selected and adopted the inventions of others. Apart from the startling 19-syllable line in 'Campoamor' and one of fifteen syllables in 'Cordura', Machado never wrote a line longer than an alexandrine. This conservatism distinguished him sharply from those Modernists, who at some point of their work extended lines almost as if to see how long they could become. However, Machado followed the new trend in cultivating shorter lines of five syllables in 'Mutis', 'Neurastenia', 'Oasis', and in groupings of *sextillas*, ababcc, in 'Es la mañana'; and, inspired as much by Verlaine as by Darío, lines of four syllables in 'Otoño' and 'El viento'.

The Modernists, as Max Henríquez Ureña observed, did not only invent new metres but gave new life and flexibility to ones already accepted, at least nominally, by the academicians. Machado in his 'Glosa' on Berceo followed Darío who had already revived the medieval stanza of mono-rhymed alexandrines in a lament for the death of José Victorio Lastarria (1888). And 'Mariposa negra' is a good example of how pliable the plain assonant *romance* could become in the hands of the Modernists. 'Última' illustrates

---

[1] See *Diario de Huelva*, 20 January 1944.

equally well how much life could be put into the old *octavilla aguda*; Amado Nervo and González Prada were among the few other Modernists to employ it. Already in *Alma* Machado used the 9-syllable line—considered by the impenitent rhetoricians as a metre with neither music nor grace, as Henríquez Ureña put it— not just in the combinations of three syllables (discussed below), but with great success in *silvas* together with lines of 7 and 11 syllables, as in 'Los días sin sol' and 'Oasis'. Again he was not the first to do this, for the 9-syllable line had already been cultivated 'con musicalidad atrayente' by José Asunción Silva in 'Estrellas', 'Égalité' and 'Avant propos' (all pre-1894) and by Julián del Casal in 'Tardes de lluvia' (1893). But Machado was original in the use he put the line to, using it precisely for the lack of music and grace which, before the Modernists' reworking of it, had made it unpopular. In Machado's work it appears most frequently during the *El Mal Poema* period, when Machado was exploring the possibilities of deliberate prosaism, in poems like 'El camino', 'A José Nogales, muerto', 'Fin', 'La canción del alba' and several others.

The sonnet, the form in which Machado most often cast his verse, is a constant throughout his work, from the beginnings in *Tristes y Alegres*, with poems like 'Al olvido' and 'Realidad', to the self-depreciatory poem he sent to *A.B.C.* very shortly before his death which was entitled 'No se libró ni el gato de un soneto ...' However, the type of sonnet he wrote was not constant. Only before *Alma* are all his sonnets classical in rhyme and length of line, and only after 1936 did they again become so in his propaganda for an orthodox Spain. In other words, his experiments coincided with his Modernism, and this, in the case of the sonnet, led to rare originality on Machado's part. For though he followed Darío in the use of the sonnet with 9-syllable lines, and although his first octosyllabic sonnet (the *sonetillo*) '"Nessun maggior dolore"' came nearly forty years after Darío's 'Para una cubana', he shared with him the distinction of endowing the Spanish language with the first example of a sonnet with mixed alexandrine and 11-syllable lines: his 'Madrid viejo' (*Caprichos*) appeared, like Darío's 'Melancolía' (*Cantos de vida y esperanza*), in 1905. And with polymetric sonnets like 'Madrigal de madrigales' (which has lines of 7, 9, 11 and 14 syllables) he was no less adventurous than Alfonso Reyes. In any case, at his experimental best, Manuel Machado was supreme in the sonnet form, as his brother Antonio recognized when he wrote, being perhaps unfair to Darío: 'La emoción del soneto se ha perdido. Queda sólo el esqueleto, demasiado sólido y pesado para la forma lírica actual. Todavía se encuentran algunos buenos sonetos en los poetas portugueses. En España son bellísimos los de Manuel Machado. Rubén Darío no hizo ningún digno de mención.'[1] If Manuel Machado did manage to revive the 'emotion of the sonnet' it was because he bent its strictness to his poetic needs, breaking the force of a central caesura and picking out secondary accents (see below), and because he allowed the sinuous rhythm of his thoughts to have its way in unexpected changes of length of line, fierce enjambments, dots and other typographical devices, as in 'Madrid viejo':

> Una plaza tranquila. Sol...Más de medio día.
> La blanca tapia de un convento...Una
> fachada de palacio antiguo...Lerma...Osuna...
> La seriedad del sitio corrige la alegría
>
> de la luz. Vana hierba entre las piedras crece.
> Rejas—las viejas lanzas de los antepasados—
> guardan los ventanales y balcones volados
> del caserón antiguo que tranquilo envejece.

Like the sonnet, the *silva* of 7- and 11-syllable lines, which abounds in *Tristes y Alegres*, was also a favourite form of Machado's: nearly a quarter of the poems in *Alma*, for example, are *silvas* of this type, and the proportion remained high in his successive collections. But, once again, after 1900 it was rarely recognizable as the same form. For in *Alma* he abandoned the classical rhyme scheme once and for all, and like Bécquer, and the Darío of *Azul...*, used assonance instead, regularly in 'El jardín gris' and 'Melancolía', and slightly irregularly in 'Madrigal'. In 'Castilla', in stanzas of the most varied length, he used the form

---

[1] 'Sobre el empleo de las imágenes en lírica,' *Obras completas* (Madrid, 1947), p. 1204.

audaciously, clustering groups of 7-, or of 11-syllable lines together for specific emotional effects. As A. Carballo Picazo has noted,[1] the longer line is generally used to express the epic force of the Cid and his men, while the slender 7-syllable line catches the delicacy and fragility of the girl who speaks to them from the doorway of the inn. The freedom of Machado's development of the *silva* in this poem, and in 'Oasis' (also of *Alma*) which in its brevity includes lines of 5 and 9 syllables, made him one of the most ambitious of the Modernists in this form, and certainly more ambitious than Darío was at that date. In fact his experiments caused Cejador y Frauca to see in 'Oasis' 'versos de ninguna especie'[2] and to condemn Machado for abusing a tendency towards free verse.

If it was an abuse, Machado showed no inclination to correct it in the period immediately after *Alma*. 'Se dice lentamente' with a very lax rhyme pattern, included in its original version lines of 3 and 5 syllables and, after revision, an alexandrine. 'Vísperas' had an even looser rhyme scheme and included lines of 4 syllables, thus forming a striking contrast with Darío's 'Helios' (*Cantos de vida y esperanza*) which also appeared in *Helios* in 1903 and had a perfectly regular rhyme scheme despite its alexandrines. Cejador y Frauca was right in pointing out the tendency towards free verse: nearly all those later poems of Machado's which are no longer restricted to any recognized verse-form can be seen nevertheless to derive from the basic *silva* of 7 and 11 syllables in *Alma*. This is unquestionably the case with 'Campoamor', those stanzas of *Ars moriendi* which Juan Ramón Jiménez published in his *Índice*, and above all the poem 'Paisaje estival' in *Phoenix*. This collection shows that Manuel Machado was powerfully affected by the innovations of a younger generation of poets, and it marks another significant change in his style. But a consistent progression is still recognizable within his work and 'Alcohol', with an occasional rhyme and lines of 4, 5, 6 and 9 syllables, and 'Madrigal

---

[1] *Notas*, p. 71; in this laboriously exhaustive study Carballo Picazo also remarks on the similarity of this poem to Antonio Machado's *silvas* in *Campos de Castilla*, and shows how Manuel incorporated phrases from the *Poema de mío Cid* into the poem.   [2] *Historia*, p. 59.

a una chica...', assonant and rhymed, with a yet greater variety of lengths of line, both show how Machado arrived at *vers libre* by being increasingly free in his use of the *silva* of 7 and 11 syllables.

In order to achieve greater freedom of expression, Machado also used increasingly elastic groupings of basic 3- or 4-syllable units. José Asunción Silva's 'Nocturno' (1894) is the generally recognized precedent for this second unit. Machado, however, seems to have modelled his 'Encajes' and other poems of the 4-syllable type less on Silva than on Darío, who did not rely so exclusively on insistent rhythmic drive as Silva did, as a comparison between the 'Nocturno' and a poem like 'Una noche tuve un sueño' indicates. In any case, with his extraordinary lightness of touch, Machado excelled both precedents: 'Figulinas', for example, prompted Juan Chabás to wonder how the Spanish language could escape so magically its heavy syntactical legacy.[1] So far as the 3-syllable unit is concerned, Machado was directly Darío's debtor. 'Marcha triunfal' (1895) is obviously the formal source of 'Versailles', which has lines of 3, 6, 9 and 12 syllables, and of 'La noche blanca', 'Copo de nieve' and 'Cordura' with its 15-syllable line. Metrically, Machado was at his freest in two poems whose inspiration is essentially dramatic, and in which a variety of metres is used to indicate the varying tempos of the action: that of a pantomime in 'Pantomima' and that of a bull-fight in *La fiesta nacional*. In the first poem groups of 3-syllable units alternate brusquely with groups of 4-syllable ones, creating the savage syncopated rhythm Machado wanted for his description of the farcical jerky movements of his characters Pierrot and Margot. Changes of tempo are not so violent in *La fiesta nacional*, which in its final form is a drawn-out and unhappy poem. The different metres in the different sections (first 4-syllable units, then 11- and 7-syllable lines, then 3-syllable units) follow each other almost predictably. The generally stale impression this poem makes, in marked contrast to 'Pantomima',

---

[1] 'El castellano danza y se quiebra y se ciñe y taconea con un donaire tan suelto, una gracia tan rizada, que a veces maravilla como pueda nuestra lengua plegarse al ligero y alado ritmo de esa poesía' (*Vuelo y estilo*, p. 105).

may be the result of its having been put together piecemeal over a period of years.[1]

A particular objective and consequence of the Modernists' assault on the rigidity of traditional poetic measures was the development of the secondary accent: a subtle, syncopated beat set off against expected emphasis. Dámaso Alonso thought this one of their most important achievements: 'Creo que una de las mayores intuiciones oscuras (si vale la expresión) que han tenido nuestros modernistas es la de la utilización con fines rítmicos de los acentos secundarios. Esta utilización, en la mayor parte de los casos, implica un ligero refuerzo del acento secundario, mejor dicho, una capacidad de seleccionar rítmicamente el acento secundario.'[2] The first example of Manuel Machado's exploitation of the secondary accent in this way occurs in *Alma*, in the poem 'Pierrot y Arlequín', from which the following extract is taken:

> Pierrot y Arlequín
> mirándose sin
> rencores,
> después de cenar
> pusiéronse a hablar
> de amores.
> Y dijo Pierrot:
> — ¿Qué buscas tú?
> — ¿Yo?...
> ¡placeres!
> — Entonces no más
> disputas por las
> mujeres.
> ....

His audacity earned the criticism of Miguel de Unamuno speaking *ex cathedra* in his prologue to *Alma. Museo. Los Cantares*.[3] 'Sin' and 'las', Unamuno argued, were obviously not the acute mono-

---

[1] Section I of the poem first appeared in *Caprichos*, under the title 'Rojo y negro'. Sections II, IV, VI and VII belong to the volume *La fiesta nacional*, but large parts of sections III and V first appeared as separate poems in *Alma. Museo. Los Cantares*. The poem was first published in its final form in *El Mal Poema*.

[2] 'Ligereza y gravedad', p. 61.

[3] He said nothing on the matter in his review of *Alma*.

syllables the Real Academia Española said they were and therefore could not stand in a position which gave them the value of 2 syllables as masculine endings. No argument can be brought against Unamuno in those terms; it is rather a question of considering the frivolous syncopated effect Machado had wanted to achieve by forcing the secondary accent and which evidently escaped Unamuno. This particular poem has a patent antecedent in Verlaine's 'Columbine' which I shall not reproduce since other critics have already quoted it. Other examples of secondary accents in Machado's poetry could however equally well derive from Darío. Compare:

> y los astros del cielo te acompañan, y los
> ramos...   ('Alma mía')

with

> un morir de deseos atropellados, y un
> matarse...   ('En la muerte de Julio Ruelas')

and

> y sufrir por la vida y por la sombra y por
> lo que...   ('Lo fatal')

with

> Y las amables sutilezas de
> una creencia...   ('¡Paz!')

The development of the secondary accent by the Modernists is most interesting when the accents are determined by the position of the caesura in an alexandrine, a matter explored with great sensitivity by Dámaso Alonso in the essay 'Ligereza y gravedad en la poesía de Manuel Machado'. Against those who, on the strength of natural breath grouping or sense alone, would claim a shift of the caesura from its central position, he argued that the nuances so dear to the Modernists were precisely a result of the syncopation between the 'natural' break and the caesura retained mercilessly in its central position. Certainly Manuel Machado himself, when discussing the metrical innovations of the Modernists,[1] spoke of their effort merely to attenuate and not to destroy the tonic accent; so that the ear could appreciate subtle syncopations and 'vagas melodías matizadas'. But the best proof of the point is

---

[1] *La Guerra Literaria*, p. 34.

Dámaso Alonso's own.[1] If, he argued, one were indeed to insist, as one critic had, on the tripartite structure of Darío's line:

'¡Oh Sor María! ¡Oh Sor María! ¡Oh Sor María!;'

and if one put caesuras between the exclamation marks, in that case the Modernists' capacity for writing alexandrines of 14 syllables would be in doubt. Clearly the only way of arriving at the correct number of syllables was to retain the central caesura and read the line thus:

¡Oh Sor María! ¡Oh Sòr : María! ¡Oh Sor María!

Unfortunately Dámaso Alonso gave neither dates nor references to the poems of Darío he used to illustrate his study, yet he concluded it by assuming that, in the matter of secondary accents, Machado faithfully followed Darío's innovations. Not only was Darío's poetry left undated; often the examples taken from Machado's poetry were by no means the first of their type to occur, and in this whole question, where the difference of a year or two may prove decisive, chronology is important.

In the simplest case of an accent forced by the caesura, Darío's precedence can easily be demonstrated. Examples occur in 'El reino interior' (1896), a poem dedicated to Eugenio de Castro whose 'Oaristos' (1890) undoubtedly influenced Darío in his use of the alexandrine:

en su blancura dè : palomas y de estrellas

But the phenomenon appears in Machado earlier than Dámaso Alonso intimated. He took lines from 'Prólogo-epílogo' (1909):

mendigo, emigra còn : la música a otra parte.

que ama las nubes y èl : dolor y la cocina.

In so doing he ignored the example in 'Adelfos', published in 1902 and written, if Machado's note 'París 1899', is to be trusted, earlier still:

En mi alma, hermana dè : la tarde, no hay contornos.

[1] 'Ligereza y gravedad', p. 65. Secondary accents are indicated by a grave accent sign.

Cases of words being cut in two by the caesura can also be found in Darío's 'El reino interior':

> Dios se refleja en è- ⋮ sos dulces alabastros

So too can cases of the part of the divided word left at the end of the first hemistich not being the normally accented syllable of that word:

> llenan el aire de hè- ⋮ chiceros beneficios

> y entre las ramas èn- ⋮ cantadas, papemores.

Again Darío was clearly first despite Tomás Navarro's opinion that Darío did not break words with the caesura until 1905, in *Cantos de vida y esperanza*.[1] It is true that examples of this use are far more numerous in that book, and their effect on Machado is patent; it will be remembered that he was very close to Darío at that time:

> La Caridad, la Cà- ⋮ ridad, la Caridad.   ('Kyrie eleyson')

of *Caprichos* is clearly influenced by Darío's '¡Oh Sor María!', and this line from Darío's preface to Valle-Inclán's *Sonata de Primavera* (1904):

> y por caso de cè- ⋮ rebración inconsciente

is a model for Machado's:

> tiene derecho a dès- ⋮ cansar y estar ahora   ('Un hidalgo')

And even in the special case of the line

> Y en una dulce ⋮ convalecencia una mañana   ('Sé buena')

Darío again anticipated Machado with:

> y los moluscos ⋮ reminiscencias de mujeres.   ('Filosofía')

Conceivably the caesura could still remain in its central position and divide the words 'convalecencia' in Machado's line and 'reminiscencias' in Darío's. But in that case '-va-' and '-mi-' would have, exceptionally, to form not a masculine, but the latter half of a feminine ending. Despite Dámaso Alonso's persuasive arguments for the retention of the caesura in a central position whatever the circumstances, here it would seem more plausible to

---

[1] *Métrica española* (New York, 1956), p. 150.

say that Darío and Machado were the first Modernists to move the caesura, at last and irremediably, and write alexandrines of 5 and 9 syllables.

Even if, as this brief examination suggests, Machado was never first to introduce a given modification to the alexandrine, nevertheless he showed rare insight in the way he adopted the modifications made by others. As Gerhard Lepiorz[1] has shown, he used them to good effect in the tercets of his sonnet 'Domingo'. First the syncopated, restless din outside his window, expressed by enjambment and the pull of the 'natural' break against the central caesura:

> Voces, gritos, canción : apenas...Bulla. Locas
> carcajadas... ¿Será : que pasa la alegría?
> Y yo aquí, solo, triste : y lejos de las fiestas...

When he asks for peace the balance of the line is restored:

> Dame, Señor, las necias : palabras de estas bocas,
> dame que suene tanto : mi risa cuando ría,
> dame un alma sencilla : como cualquiera de éstas.

Machado also displayed the technique of a Modernist in the way he used rhyme. The only opinion he expressed on this subject, late in life, is misleading:

> Para mí, la rima no es sólo el elemento poético que opera, en orden a la memoria y a lo que pudiéramos llamar la temporalización del poema, sino también a su personalización. Es, a veces, el poema todo.[2]

He went on to speak of his preference for full rhyme, 'la rima consonante': 'No creo en el fondo que haya otra, pues la asonante, empleada sobre todo por el pueblo, no es sino la persecución—que se queda en el camino—de la más completa y perfecta, a la que siempre tiende, si lo observamos bien.' This opinion, uttered at the height of the Civil War, was accepted as representative of Manuel Machado's ideas by Alfredo Carballo[3] and contrasted

[1] *Symbolismus*, p. 50. Lepiorz saw in 'Domingo' an example of more adventurous enjambment than Darío had used by that date (1907). In fact Darío had gone even further in that direction in *Prosas profanas* when he broke a word in two: 'Al lado izquierdo y paralela-mente,'. Lepiorz interpreted the alexandrine traditionally and therefore did not feel the syncopation of the first tercet.

[2] *Unos versos*, p. 73   [3] *Notas*, p. 72.

with Antonio's preference for assonance. There may be here a good example of the intimate connexion between poetry and politics; but from any point of view Machado's *volte-face*, is curious. While his taste for formal structure and full rhyme was amply evident in the verse he wrote as a propagandist after 1936, before that date he had tended increasingly, in all but his 'obras de encargo', towards free verse and the loosest of assonance. Well over half the poems in *Alma*, and all the *silvas*, are assonant. Naturally it is not a matter of suggesting that Machado, or any other Modernist, scorned rhyme absolutely. In his account of *La Guerra Literaria*, he emphasized the Modernists' struggle to break away, not from rhyme altogether, but from obligatory and hackneyed rhymes, 'la rima consabida'.[1] The Modernists were determined that if they were to use full rhyme and regular metre they were going to use them and not be used by them. Generally they shrank from making rhyme the whole essence of a serious poem in the way recommended by the older Manuel Machado, and used it rather to produce particular effects.

Darío's virtuoso displays of internal rhyme indicated a new attitude to rhyme itself:

> Mía: así te llamas.
> ¿Qué más harmonía?
> Mía: luz del día;
> Mía: rosas, llamas. ('Mía')

and:

> Con negros ojos
> vío la manzana del jardín: con labios
> rojos probó su miel; con labios rojos
> que saben hoy más ciencia que los sabios.
> ('Alaba los ojos negros de Julia')

Machado echoed this frivolity in 'Rosa...', a poem he called 'un juguetillo sin importancia':

> Labios sabios, Rosa loca,
> ¿sabes que
> saben mucho más tus labios
> de todo lo que yo sé?

[1] *Ibid.* p. 32.

On receiving the copy of *Caprichos* Machado sent him, Darío added stanzas to 'Rosa...' in his own hand.[1] Like many others, the incident serves to show an affinity—and to make a distinction. The stanzas Darío added lacked much of the lightness and inconsequence of Machado's original; the joke, taken too far, was not funny any more. Too often Darío's almost childlike delight in internal rhymes led him to abuse them, as for instance in 'Ite, missa est':

> Su risa es la sonrisa suave de Monna Lisa,

or 'Palabras de la satiresa':

> vi brotar de lo verde dos manzanas lozanas;
> erectos senos eran las lozanas manzanas.

Machado was generally more discreet. Excesses of internal rhyme and jangling 'rimas consabidas' can certainly be found in his poetry:

> La voluntad... ¡Es verdad!
> ....
>
> borra montes, seca pontos...
> Yo no he visto más que tontos
> que tuvieran voluntad.   ('Última')

and:

> Poema sin embargo,
> de rima consabida;
> pocma largo, largo,
> ¡como una mala vida!...   ('Prosa')

In both cases, however, the use is obviously deliberate and intended to express not just the poet's spleen but dissatisfaction with the normal 'poetic' methods of expressing spleen; and ultimately perhaps a refusal to take even that dissatisfaction seriously.

At the other extreme, as Dámaso Alonso has shown,[2] Machado could employ internal rhyme as a subtle 'remate' to a sonnet:

> Mas ella jamás ha retornado
> como retornan ¡siempre! mayo gentil y abril.   ('La primavera')

---

[1] Manuel Machado, 'Rubén y Yo', *Arriba*, 5 February 1946. Machado's article was prompted by another (which I have not seen) by the director of *Arte y letras* who first found the copy of *Caprichos* 'en el cual Rubén Darío había escrito de su puño y letra la continuación de algunas composiciones'. In his article Machado published Darío's additions to 'Rosa...', and made further additions of his own.

[2] 'Ligereza y gravedad', p. 66.

Or in the magnificent final tercet of 'Felipe IV':

> Y, en vez de cetro real, sostiene apenas,
> con desmayo galán, un guante de ante
> la blanca mano de azuladas venas.

This last example is interesting because normally the embarrassment of being left with an unpaired line in the last tercet of a poem in terza rima (aba, bcb, cdc) is avoided by the addition of a fourth line to match the second (aba, bcb, cdcd). Machado, so ingeniously that few notice his ingenuity, used internal rhyme.

The Modernists brought many other elements into Spanish poetry which could also be conveniently discussed in terms of prosody. Carlos Bousoño has already indicated, in his analysis of 'La corte' and 'Oriente', the importance of Machado's methods of indirect suggestion, of avoiding direct statement and leaving a row of dots to say what has been left unsaid.[1] More generally, a description of Machado's 'Mariposa negra' or 'Madrid viejo' for instance could lead to further observations on the Modernists' attempt to loosen syntax and their technique of linking ideas in free association between groups of dots. However, what has been said already must serve as a basis for the conclusion that the technical resources Machado had at his disposal after he had become conscious of being a Modernist far exceeded those he possessed before that date, and that at the turn of the century his whole style of writing altered as a result. Since it is important for the following chapter, perhaps it ought to be emphasized that though Machado learnt a great deal through Darío, on occasion he appears to have taken a short cut directly to French sources. Lastly he was remarkable for the speed with which he assimilated 'la poesía nueva', for the way he discarded its excesses and took advantage of its richer possibilities.

[1] *Teoría*, p. 75.

9

MODERNISM WITHIN MODERNISM

Warning critics against interpreting the word Modernism narrowly, Federico de Onís mentioned Darío's name specifically: 'A menudo se cae en este error cuando la denominación de modernismo se aplica exclusivamente al tipo de poesía caracterizado por ciertas formas y espíritu que puso en circulación Rubén Darío, sin pensar que no son características ni exclusivas de este autor siquiera.'[1] In his assessment of Manuel Machado's debt to Darío, Dámaso Alonso appeared to commit this very error by attributing extraordinary importance to the publication of *Prosas profanas*. Referring to all that was new in Machado's work and indeed in Spanish poetry as a whole he said: 'Todo esto, todo, nace directa e indirectamente de las *Prosas profanas*, de Rubén Darío, e indirectamente del contacto por medio de él con toda la poesía francesa del siglo XIX, desde Hugo, pasando por los parnasianos, hasta los simbolistas.'[2] Shortly afterwards, however, in the same essay, Dámaso Alonso attenuated this 'todo' in the case of Manuel Machado: 'Pero no vamos a distinguir aquí lo que le vino por el canal de Rubén Darío de lo que él bebió directamente en su estancia en París.'[3] Even so, Juan Ramón Jiménez shifted the emphasis still further away from Darío. As far as the symbolists were concerned, he said that the Machados and he were never Darío's debtors; on the contrary Darío owed something to them:

Nosotros leímos a Verlaine antes de que lo leyera Darío. Le conocimos directamente, en los originales. Fíjese que en *Azul*...no se cita a Verlaine; allí están Catulle Mendès, Leconte de Lisle, Richepin...En nosotros, en los Machado y en mí, los simbolistas influyeron antes que en Darío. Los Machado los leyeron cuando su estancia en París, y yo presté a Darío libros de Verlaine que él aun no conocía.[4]

[1] *Antología*, p. xiv.   [2] 'Ligereza y gravedad', p. 53.
[3] *Ibid.* p. 54.   [4] R. Gullón, *Conversaciones*, p. 56.

The purpose of this chapter is to try and reconcile these opinions in order to assess Manuel Machado's role as an innovator. This will involve examining his relation to Darío and to other poets thought by their contemporaries to have been innovators in their own right, and hence suggesting that Modernist groups, each with their own characteristics, existed within the movement as a whole in Spain.

To take first a point generally agreed on, that Darío was responsible for introducing nineteenth-century French poets prior to the Symbolists into Spain. The case of Leconte de Lisle is not problematic: Machado may well have first sensed the tense atmosphere of the *Poèmes barbares* in Darío's poetry. The burning sand, the lion and the elastic tiger of 'Oasis' can all be found in *Azul...* and *Prosas profanas*. However, the closeness of Machado's 'Oasis' to Leconte de Lisle's 'L'Oasis' and 'Le désert'[1] is striking: the details of the Arab resting by the palm trees, about to be attacked by a tiger, are not echoed so exactly by Darío. The other patent example of Leconte de Lisle's influence on Machado in *Alma* is interesting and ironic, ironic because so much has been said about the true Spanishness of 'Castilla'. In fact the parallels of Machado's poem with the Frenchman's 'L'accident de Don Iñigo'[2] are hard to ignore. Compare:

> El ciego sol se estrella
> en las duras aristas de las armas
> llaga de luz petos y espaldares
> y flamea en las puntas de las lanzas.

with

> Seul, Rui Diaz de Vivar enfourche, roide et fier,
> son cheval de bataille enchemisé de fer.
> Il a l'estoc, la lance, et la cotte maillée
> qui de la nuque aux reins reluit ensoleillée,
> et, pour garer le casque aux reflets aveuglants,
> ....

Again:

> ¡Quema el sol, el aire abrasa!

with

> Vers midi, dans la plaine où l'air poussiéreux brûle.

[1] *Poèmes barbares.* [2] *Poèmes barbares.*

Leconte de Lisle's Cid rides 'à travers les champs pierreux qui n'ont point d'ombre' and Machado's 'por la terrible estepa castellana'. The two poems even end in a similar way:

> Una voz inflexible grita: '¡En marcha!'
> ···············
> al destierro, con doce de los suyos,
> — polvo, sudor y hierro — el Cid cabalga.

> Puis, sans s'inquiéter qu'on le blâme ou poursuive,
> avec ses fidalgos, devers Calatrava,
> le bon Campeador tourne bride et s'en va.

Between this poem and Machado's stands Darío's 'Cosas del Cid',[1] which Darío freely admitted was in turn inspired by Barbey d'Aurevilly. Darío provided the other character in Machado's poem, the girl and the sentimental softness associated with her:

> A los terribles golpes,
> de eco ronco, una voz pura, de plata
> y de cristal responde...Hay una niña
> muy débil y muy blanca
> en el umbral. Es toda
> ojos azules y en los ojos lágrimas.

In Darío's poem she appeared

> vestida de inocencia,
> una niña que fuera una mujer, de franca
> y angélica pupila, y muy dulce y muy blanca.

The influence of Leconte de Lisle's disciple J. M. de Hérédia, evident in *Prosas profanas*, is still easier to detect in *Alma*. Darío was never so close to Hérédia as Machado was in 'Oriente' which, translated, could almost have been included in the section of *Les Trophées* dedicated to 'Antoine et Cléopâtre'. But there is no conclusive proof that in the case of the poets prior to the Symbolists Darío did not fulfil the intermediary role assigned to him by all critics.

The question of the French Symbolists is altogether more complicated. Darío was undoubtedly influential in achieving a whole revolution of taste and new attitudes in Spain towards contem-

---

[1] *Prosas profanas*; although one of the 'adiciones de 1901', 'Cosas del Cid' first appeared 30 March 1900, i.e. well before 'Castilla'.

porary French poetry. But this change of attitude has not been exhaustively documented, even in the case of a poet of the stature of Baudelaire. In his preface to *Los raros* Darío may have claimed to have been the only important propagator of Symbolism, yet in the book he discussed minor figures like Dubus and Hannon in preference to Rimbaud, Mallarmé and Laforgue. Furthermore, some of the articles on which Darío based his claim, those on Castro and Martí for instance, were obviously written later than he said. A full discussion of this question would be out of proportion here and so the problem of literary precedence will be mentioned only when it is strictly relevant to the poetry Manuel Machado wrote at the beginning of the century.

Juan Ramón's claim that he and the Machados told Darío about Verlaine is improbable. Even if (as Jiménez pointed out) Verlaine's name is absent from *Azul...*, his influence is evident enough in *Prosas profanas*. Besides Verlaine was generally known about in literary circles in Madrid after A. Sawa's return from Paris in 1896. On the other hand on the basis of textual evidence alone it is difficult to prove that Machado took much from Verlaine independently of Darío before the publication of *Alma*, that is, before his second visit to Paris. The atmosphere of 'Versailles' and more specifically Machado's picture of Watteau's princess[1] could have been copied from Verlaine or from Darío. Again it could be argued that Machado's Pierrot and Columbina ('La noche blanca', 'Copo de nieve') were taken from Darío's 'Canción de carnaval' and 'El faisán',[2] although Machado's frivolity is closer to Verlaine's and Darío's quotation from Banville suggests an earlier source for 'Canción de carnaval'.[3] Only 'Otoño'[4] and 'Felipe IV' indicate that Machado knew Verlaine better than Darío. The second of these, the first of the portrait poems Machado

---

[1] 'Figulinas'; compare 'si ella ríe, río yo' (l. 10) with 'la divina Eulalia ríe, ríe ríe' ('Era un aire suave...').

[2] *Prosas profanas*.

[3] See E. K. Mapes, *L'influence française dans l'œuvre de Rubén Darío* (Paris 1925), pp. 70–1; this point is argued more closely than the case for the influence, in general, of Baudelaire, Rimbaud and Mallarmé (pp. 78–86).

[4] I do not reproduce the relevant passage from 'Otoño' because other critics, notably Dámaso Alonso in 'Ligereza y gravedad', have discussed it already.

introduced into Spain, apparently without the help of Darío, reminded Unamuno of Leconte de Lisle.[1] Díez-Canedo was more exact and perceptive when he said 'se parece más a "César Borgia" que a todo Leconte de Lisle'.[2] Indeed the following lines from Verlaine's portrait, translated by Machado, are remarkably close to 'Felipe IV':

> (los) cabellos negros, y el negro terciopelo,
> contrastan, entre el oro suntuoso de la tarde,
> con la palidez bella y mate de su rostro.[3]

The whole question is further complicated by the fact that during his first trip to Paris, when he made the acquaintance of French poets, personally and through their books, Machado also lived in close contact with Darío. On present evidence it would seem unwise to say more than this: that even though Darío knew more of Verlaine than Juan Ramón claimed he knew, still, before the end of 1901 Verlaine's influence on his style seems less profound than on that of Manuel Machado. Similarly, while *Prosas profanas* was undoubtedly an important book, Machado's poetry was unaffected after its publication and changed only after his stay in Paris.

The style of the poems published in *Helios* and *Blanco y Negro* after his second visit to Paris is evidence in support of Juan Ramón's claim, on another occasion, that everything had changed again by 1902: 'Menos Villaespesa, todo había cambiado en aquellos años. Ahora rejían los simbolistas y Góngora. Yo traje de Francia libros y revistas que desaparecieron de mano en mano.'[4] By 1903 the direct influence of Verlaine on Machado is irrefutable. The example of 'Pierrot y Arlequín', discussed earlier, suffices. 'Tiene Manuel Machado influencias bien aprovechadas de Verlaine y de Albert Samain; de este último en la dicción y la construcción sobre todo.'[5] The prominence Juan Ramón gave to this statement, the opening sentence of his essay on Machado, suggests that he may have played a part in drawing his attention at least to Samain. The influence is there, clearly enough, in

---

[1] 'El *Alma* de Manuel Machado'. See also Chapter 11 below.
[2] Review of *Poesías escogidas*, p. 5.   [3] *Fiestas galantes*, p. 76.
[4] *La corriente*, p. 67.   [5] *Ibid.* p. 41.

'Abel', published at the end of 1903. Compare these lines from 'La peau de bête':

> Le jour allait finir; à l'horizon livide
> l'œil rouge du soleil palpitait dans du sang.
> Les ombres s'allongeaient dans le soir menaçant
> et la terre était nue, et le ciel était vide.[1]

with:

> El campo y el crepúsculo. Una hoguera
> cuyo humo lentamente al cielo sube.
> En la pálida esfera
> no hay una sola nube.

Or

> Et la nuit descendait sur eux comme la mort

with

> Y baja como un duelo soberano
> la noche a la pradera.

These examples of Machado's closeness to the original French, and of the role both he and Jiménez played in making the Symbolists better known after 1902, serve to correct the impression that all the currents which flowed into Modernism flowed in exclusively through Darío.

In any fair account of 'la nueva poesía' in *Alma*, at least one other force[2] must be reckoned with: Francisco Villaespesa. At the turn of the century Villaespesa was in touch with most of the Modernists in Latin America,[3] and with a number of Portuguese poets;

---

[1] *Œuvres*, Paris, Mercure de France, 1924, II, p. 197.

[2] Of course writers like Salvador Rueda were also important as Modernist innovators, but there is no incontestable proof of their influence on Machado and therefore they fall outside the scope of this chapter. It is curious that Machado should have had so little contact with Catalan Modernism. He met Guimerá in Barcelona as a young man (cf. *Un año*, pp. 255-6) but denied him the importance G. Díaz-Plaja attributes him (*Modernismo*, p. 337); he contributed neither to *Vida nueva* nor to *Arte joven*, the two reviews in Madrid most concerned with Barcelona, and no Catalan is the object of a dedication in *Alma*.

[3] Villaespesa's importance as a link between Spanish American and Spanish Modernists has been emphasized by Juan Ramón Jiménez: 'Villaespesa devoraba la literatura hispanoamericana...Libros que entonces reputábamos joyas misteriosas y que en realidad eran y son libros de valor, unos más y otros menos, los tenía él, sólo él; *Ritos*, de Guillermo Valencia, *Castalia bárbara*, de Ricardo Jaimes Freyre, *Cuentos de color*, de Manuel Díaz Rodríguez, *Los crepúsculos del jardín*, de Leopoldo Lugones, *Perlas negras*, de Amado Nervo' (*La corriente*,

the dedication in *Alma* to Silvio Rebello, for example, who wrote
for the *Revista Nova* in Lisbon, was doubtless due to a suggestion
of Villaespesa's. While the question has not been studied thor-
oughly, it seems likely that Machado thus received ideas from
abroad which were not necessarily identical to those of Rubén
Darío. Though Juan Ramón said, and was in a sense right, that
everything had changed by 1902, yet Villaespesa and Manuel
Machado were called, that very year, the only two Spanish poets
worthy of the name of Symbolists.[1] In fact Villaespesa's Symbolism, or that curious and original verse of *La copa del rey de Thule*
and *El alto de los bohemios*, was a powerful force on Manuel
Machado and all those who worked together at Fuencarral
throughout 1901 and read out their poems for criticism by the
others. Much of Villaespesa's verse may have been rehashed
Spanish Romanticism, but it was Romanticism tinged with the
colours of the French Symbolists. At times he echoed a Symbolist
directly. For example, when commenting on Machado's poem 'El
jardín negro', González Blanco wrote of its 'hálito de misterio'
and 'una ráfaga de Maeterlinckismo', and, ignoring Villaespesa,
described this as a new element in Spanish poetry.[2] Yet 'El jardín
negro' has an obvious precedent in Villaespesa's 'Los murciélagos'.[3]
In both poems 'la amada' huddles frightened against her lover's
chest; Villaespesa has the wing of a bat brush their foreheads:

> De repente, nuestras frentes rozó el ala
> de un fatídico murciélago.

The lover in Machado's poem shudders

> como si rozado
> me hubiera un momento
> el ala peluda
> de horrible murciélago...

pp. 70–1). The general influence of these works is obvious, for example, in the
coincidence of such titles as 'País de sombra' (Jaimes Freyre), 'Paisaje de sombra'
(Villaespesa) and 'Estatuas de sombra' (Machado). For Valencia, see below,
p. 120.
[1] Gonzalo Guasp, quoted by Díaz-Plaja, *Modernismo*, p. 38.
[2] *Los contemporáneos*, p. 114.
[3] *La copa del rey de Thule* (Madrid, 1900), p. 55. At the time Machado said he was
drunk with this cup (F. de Cossío, 'Vieja poesía que fue nueva', *A.B.C.*, 27 May
1960).

Villaespesa's more sensational poetry, ably copied by Juan Ramón in work he later disowned or altered out of recognition, soon seemed disgusting to a more refined sensibility, and with poetic justice Villaespesa was forgotten because he was once so important. The Machados however never revelled in the morbid filth on which Villaespesa's 'lívidos gusanos' thrived, nor did they indulge in the self-pity which complemented that horror.

A good example of the sort of influence exerted on Manuel Machado by Villaespesa can be found in the poem 'Mariposa negra'. Here Villaespesa was not so much the source as the catalyst which helped Machado to make a Modernist poem out of an adolescent one. For 'Oriental', also a ballad, has the same basic situation as the later 'Mariposa negra': a woman waiting anxiously for her warrior lover to return. Machado even took a stanza from his earlier poem and added it to the new one where, no longer part of a narrative, it charges the atmosphere with foreboding. In 'Oriental' the moon tells the girl her lover is dead; in 'Mariposa negra' Machado gives no more than a hint: the sun setting, 'guerrero herido en el campo', and then the stanza taken from 'Oriental' as a conclusion:

> ¡Malhayan los servidores
> que sin su señor tornaron,
> los que con él se partieron
> y traen sin él su caballo!

In this poem Machado showed he had learnt from Villaespesa how to create mood by means of indirect suggestion, in the fashion of the Symbolists. The black butterfly, the horrible beggar which Machado introduces into this later poem as omens are, like the bats, commonplace in Villaespesa's poetry. His 'Canción de la esperanza'[1] has the same basic theme as Machado's two poems except that more than one princess waits in the castle. They wait 'con los ojos siempre fijos / en el polvo del camino'; Machado's princess says: 'Nada veo, sino el polvo / del camino'. When commenting on 'Mariposa negra', González Blanco remarked that Machado had described the sunset with 'una metáfora muy nueva

---

[1] *La copa*, p. 69.

entre la agrupación de lugares comunes vesperales'.[1] He was referring to the opening stanza:

> La hora cárdena...La Tarde
> los velos se va quitando...
> El velo de oro..., el de plata;
> La hora cárdena...

Francisco Villaespesa could fairly be said to be behind this metaphor as well. He tended even to abuse the adjective 'cárdeno' when he was wanting to stimulate a sense of uneasiness; and then in 'La canción de la esperanza' the princesses had watched their lovers depart 'bajo el trueno de oro y plata' of the war trumpets. Machado's poem is altogether more finely developed than Villaespesa's, but these and other coincidences suggest that in the first place Villaespesa, more than any other Spanish poet, taught Machado the tricks of the Symbolists.

There are many other echoes of Villaespesa in the poetry both the Machados wrote at the beginning of the century and which clearly owes little to Darío. The case of Antonio Machado's recasting of Villaespesa's spinning song and his similarly impossible description of a distaff has been studied in some detail.[2] But the case of the spinning song was not isolated; rather it was one of a number of common themes: distant violins, children's voices, the fountain, the 'plegaria' in the holy hush of evening, the peace of the deserted square, the old park. Perhaps it is not generally realized how close Manuel and Antonio were to each other at this period when writing on these themes. Compare for instance lines of the 1902 version of Manuel's 'Se dice lentamente' with stanzas of Antonio's 'Yo escucho las coplas' as they first appeared that same year in *Soledades*; the theme of the monotonous, bitter-sweet music of the fountain is common to them both and similarly expressed:

Yo no sé más que una	Yo escucho las coplas
vaguísima oración,	de viejas cadencias,
una oración	que los niños cantan

---

[1] *Los contemporáneos*, p. 108.
[2] D. Alonso, 'Poesías olvidadas de Antonio Machado', *Poetas españoles contemporáneos*, p. 103.

de pena	en las tardes lentas
está y de encanto llena,	de lento verano,
y tiene llanto y risa,	....
....	....
Se dice lentamente	cual vierten sus aguas
con palabras vulgares,	las fuentes de piedra:
repetidas,	con monotonías
muy oídas...	de risas eternas,
....	que no son alegres,
y es su son	con lágrimas viejas,
—como en las soledades	que no son amargas
del campo el de la fuente—	....
monótono. (M. Machado)	(A. Machado)

Manuel's 'Vísperas', with its ancient church, white wall, old trees and lonely square, is no less akin to a poem of Antonio's published in the same number of *Helios* (October 1903), also under the title 'Vísperas':

Era una tarde quieta	A la desierta plaza
de paz. La plazoleta,	conduce un laberinto de callejas.
solitaria	A un lado, el viejo paredón sombrío
....	de una ruinosa iglesia;
El blanco se amortigua	a otro lado, la tapia blanquecina
del muro, con la sombra	de un huerto de cipreses y palmeras,
que crece de la antigua	....
iglesia, de las ramas	
de los árboles viejos	
que están allí...	
(M. Machado)	(A. Machado)

Ricardo Gullón, who has written so much about this period, has suggested that not only the Machados but the whole early group, Villaespesa, Juan Ramón Jiménez, Valle-Inclán and Martínez Sierra, expressed their nostalgia by means of a number of set scenes or devices common to them all: 'El crepúsculo, la bruma, el parque viejo, la callecita solitaria y silenciosa, la lluvia monótona, la fuente, canciones infantiles, voces lejanas, lo indeciso y vago, cuanto podía sugerir estados de ánimo melancólicos y nostálgicos fue utilizado por los modernistas.'[1] Sr. Gullón's description serves to emphasize two points made earlier. First, that

[1] 'Relaciones...entre Juan Ramón Jiménez y los Martínez Sierra'.

the term 'Modernism' is often used in a narrower sense than the one established in Chapter 6 above, for Darío is clearly a Modernist in that broad sense but not in this narrow one. Secondly, that many Modernists in Spain, Villaespesa, the Machados, Valle-Inclán, did not owe everything to Darío. Only if this is taken into account can Juan Ramón's famous remark have any meaning; for Juan Ramón, who begged Darío to collaborate in *Helios* in 1903, also said, without fearing a contradiction: 'En realidad, mi relación con Villaespesa había terminado, 1902, con mi modernismo.'[1]

Some attention has been paid to the way Antonio Machado developed the essential themes of his mature poetry from the Modernism and Symbolism of his early work. Professor Ribbans has convincingly demonstrated how the erotic fountain and the sentimental 'Parque viejo' of the *Electra* group, adopted from Verlaine, were adapted to the needs of an austere and exacting poet.[2] Manuel Machado's poetry never developed in this way. If anything, it tended to disintegrate after *Alma*. As Juan Ramón said, 'en *Alma*, Manuel Machado apareció formado por completo'. But within *Alma*, Manuel's treatment of Modernist material on occasion proved him to have been a maturer poet than his brother at that time. For example Ricardo Gullón's account of Manuel's 'El jardín gris' is not altogether fair. He began by saying, rightly, that this poem (which first appeared in *Electra* as 'El jardín viejo') had passed 'inadvertido por los comentaristas'.[3] But he went on to dismiss it by implication, by including it in a generalization about the 'Parque viejo' theme, a theme 'de los más característicos y definidores del modernismo'. Now Sr. Gullón had shown that he associated this 'Modernist' theme with sad and nostalgic states of mind. Admittedly Antonio Machado qualified excellently as such a Modernist:

> ...La hiedra asomaba
> al muro del parque, negra y polvorienta...
> Lejana una fuente sonaba;[4]

[1] *La corriente*, p. 68.
[2] 'La influencia de Verlaine en Antonio Machado.'
[3] 'Relaciones...entre Juan Ramón Jiménez y Manuel Machado.'
[4] 'Fue una clara tarde', *Soledades*.

and so did Juan Ramón, who published his 'Parque viejo' also in 1902. Like Antonio Machado he entered the park sad and nostalgic:

> Me he asomado por la verja
> del viejo parque desierto:
> todo parece sumido
> en un nostálgico sueño.

All the elements are there; the fountain and even a nightingale:

> El jardín vuelve a sumirse
> en melancólico sueño
> y un ruiseñor, dulce y alto,
> jime en el hondo silencio.[1]

Manuel Machado's poem is explicitly opposed to that atmosphere of sadness and nostalgia. In his garden no wind rustles in the leaves ('tus árboles no agita el viento'); no nightingale sings ('el pájaro no se posa en tus ramas'); the water does not tell the monotonous story of the fountain but lies stagnant and dead. Even the clinging ivy of Antonio's poem is something more than mere background. Unlike other Modernists Manuel Machado was not here trying to break open reservoirs of maudlin reminiscence; in his garden there was not one voice, neither memories nor hope. The more the poem is examined the clearer it becomes why Machado insisted so deliberately on the harsh, voiceless 'jota' and why he changed the 'no mueve el viento' of the first version to 'no agita el viento'. He was not at all concerned with sensuous, or as has been suggested, impressionist, description.[2] The colours in the poem do not evoke a mood but express an idea; the white of the white paths is, for instance, a recurrent symbol in his early poetry for an existentialist notion of cosmic hostility and barrenness, more fully examined in the next chapter.

The example of 'El jardín gris' shows why it is dangerous to describe Manuel Machado as a Modernist unless that word has all the breadth of meaning suggested initially. For while certain

---

[1] *Segunda antología poética* (Madrid, 1959), pp. 16–17.

[2] A. González-Blanco said 'recuerda los cuadros impresionistas de Rusiñol' (*Los contemporáneos*, p. 108). Machado's poem has nothing in common with Rusiñol's sensuous descriptions of the exquisite remnants of Spain's glory, as Machado's own interpretation of these pictures shows ('Granada, por Rusiñol').

poems in *Alma* illustrate some Modernist tendencies within Modernism as a whole—here a debt to Darío, there one to Verlaine, there another to Villaespesa—Machado cannot be exclusively identified with any one of them. Further, were it possible to account for Machado's *Alma* solely in terms of influences and common themes, clearly he would then be unworthy of even that little attention he has received as an original poet.

10

'ALMA'

'You see it rolls in us just as the other rolls—the black river of corruption. And all our flowers are of this—our sea-born Aphrodite, all our white phosphorescent flowers of sensuous perfection, all our reality, nowadays.'
'You mean that Aphrodite is really deathly?' asked Ursula.
—D. H. Lawrence, *Women in Love*

The book *Alma* lacks any obvious unity, apart from being Modernist in the broad sense. Yet its title is not entirely unindicative: a definite and close interconnection can be seen between precisely those poems in which the word 'alma' is most in evidence, those poems which in Gómez de Baquero's phrase represent 'un vuelo al psique donde cantan voces lejanas de lo subconsciente'.[1] 'Adelfos' and the poems Machado grouped under the significant heading of 'El reino interior' and 'Estatuas de sombra' are most representative of what other critics have called his psychological poetry.

In turning his attention to the subconscious, 'el reino interior', and describing 'una realidad espiritual'[2] Machado was following the poetic movement of the time away from the soul-less world of the Positivists, reacting particularly against his father's Haeckelian monism.[3] José Enrique Rodó, who thought of himself as a Modernist in this sense and, in *Ariel*, lamented the loss of spiritual values to a materialist monism, described the inner citadel of the soul in metaphors strikingly similar to those of the Modernists' poetry:

Pero dentro, muy dentro; aislada del alcázar ruidoso por cubiertos canales; oculta a la mirada vulgar—como la 'perdida iglesia' de Uhland en lo esquivo del bosque—al cabo de ignorados senderos, una misteriosa sala se extendía,...
En el ambiente flotaba como una onda indisipable la casta esencia del nenúfar, el perfume sugeridor del adormecimiento penseroso y de la contemplación

---

[1] 'El *Ars Moriendi* de M. Machado.'   [2] *Unos versos*, p. 79.
[3] Cf. p. 78 above.

del propio ser. Graves cariátides custodiaban las puertas de marfil en la actitud del silenciario. En los testeros, esculpidas imágenes hablaban de idealidad, de ensimismamiento, de reposo...[1]

Those statues which spoke of inner concentration are readily recognizable as Machado's 'Estatuas de sombra', the phrase he thought of using as a title for *Alma*;[2] the trance-like state of 'Eleusis' was similarly associated in Machado's mind with the soothing scent of flowers...lilies, spikenards, myrtle and the oleander.

For retreating into an inner citadel and preferring his dreams to reality, Machado was criticized as an escapist, like those writers whose self-obsessed isolation was examined by Edmund Wilson in *Axel's Castle*. Under a confessedly abhorrent regenerationist impulse, Unamuno even tried to excuse this aspect of Machado's poetry: he armed the dream-figure Gerineldos with exemplariness, making him a symbol of social redemption. Out of the union of the refined, cretinous aristocrat (the queen) with the peasant brutalized by poverty (Gerineldos), he argued, would spring a new human kind.[3] Concern with social problems has led some critics to consider the whole Modernist movement as a perverse turning-aside from a painful political reality: for Pedro Salinas, Machado's poem 'Adelfos' was the most perfect expression of this defeatism, this 'leaden acquiescence in defeat':

Convencidos por la derrota del '98 de la corrupción política y de la decadencia social en general, en lugar de alzarse, en son de guerra y campaña de regeneración, prefirieron entregarse al gran narcótico que les ofrecía el modernismo. La poesía de Rubén Darío y sus seguidores podía servir como una maravillosa muralla de irrealidades y placeres de la imaginación que aislara al

[1] *Ariel* (1900); the subsequent development of Rodó's thesis is of course irrelevant to this chapter. Here I wanted only to indicate once again the importance of the evolution of science in relation to Modernism. When writing on Darío, Rodó was quite explicit: 'Yo soy un *modernista* también; yo pertenezco con toda mi alma a la gran reacción que da carácter y sentido a la evolución del pensamiento en las postrimerías de esto siglo; a la reacción que, partiendo del naturalismo literario y del positivismo filosófico, los conduce a disolverse en concepciones más altas' (*Obras completas*, Montevideo, 1956, II, pp. 101–2).

[2] The poems he published in *Electra* were said to be 'Del libro en prensa *Estatuas de sombra*'.

[3] 'El *Alma* de Manuel Machado'; he was referring to the poems 'Gerineldos, el paje' and 'Lirio'.

escritor de las aflicciones inmediatas que lo rodeaban. 'Adelfos'—para mí el más perfecto ejemplo de ese derrotismo espiritual enmascarado de exquisitez literaria. La verdad es que la voluntad de muchos jóvenes españoles había enfermado gravemente, si no muerto, al choque brutal de la derrota. Pero Manuel Machado se evade de reconocer este origen de la abulia contemporánea en el desastre nacional y se lo pone en cuenta a ese pretexto romántico modernista de la noche de luna, utilizando un recurso de tramoya literaria para aislarse de la penosa realidad circunstancial.[1]

Several obvious and immediate objections can be made to this sort of sociology of literature. Were the Spanish American Modernists just as 'escapist'? In that case how are we to explain the vogue Modernism enjoyed before the war between the United States and Spain even began? What are those pleasures of the imagination to which the Modernists 'surrendered themselves' if they are not those of any lyric poet? And does writing poetry necessarily preclude other activities or other kinds of writing? A fundamental and useful objection to Salinas's type of approach was made by Manuel Machado himself when he said that he was tired of hearing that:

la moderna poesía ha de ser fuerte, con voces de aliento para las grandes revoluciones, todavía latentes; que hay que cantar las luchas sociales, las catástrofes religiosas...y que lo propio de la juventud son bríos, entusiastas y atrevimientos varoniles. Que la vida reclama sus poetas, y que no los encuentra porque ellos se encierran en la torre de marfil de los ensueños...

He defended the right of poets to write what they liked, using a word very much of the period (and in some contexts synonymous with 'alma'), 'personalidad':

Todo esto es música celestial y ganas de no enterarse. Poesía es lo que los poetas quieren. Detrás de un libro hay un artista, un hombre, una personalidad, o no hay nada. Cuando lo hay el libro interesa y no es preciso pedirle más.[2]

It is true that even in these—his own—terms, Manuel Machado was not always above reproach, not always 'interesting' as a human personality. Certain irritating fashions of the period are embarrassingly obvious in the arrogant aestheticism of 'Oliveretto

[1] *Literatura española, Siglo XX* (Mexico, 1944), pp. 36–7.
[2] From his review of J. R. Jiménez's *Rimas* (1902), published by R. Gullón, 'Relaciones...entre Juan Ramón Jiménez y Manuel Machado'.

de Fermo' ('asesino elegante y discreto'), the slushy sensuality of
'Gerineldos, el paje' and the overbearing 'décadence' of 'Adelfos':

> Yo soy como las gentes que a mi tierra vinieron
> —soy de la raza mora, vieja amiga del Sol—
> que todo lo ganaron y todo lo perdieron.
> Tengo al alma de nardo del árabe español.
>
> ....
>
> De mi alta aristocracia, dudar jamás se pudo.
> No se ganan, se heredan, elegancia y blasón...
> Pero el lema de casa, el mote del escudo,
> es una nube vaga que eclipsa un vano sol.

Aristocratic disdain, African fatalism (anathema to Unamuno and
Ortega), which expressed, for some, the mood of a defeated
Spain, and which was more particularly a reaction against
Machado y Álvarez's progressive Evolutionism: 'Entre el ángel
que cae estúpidamente y el mono que sábiamente se levanta; entre
el que todo lo tiene y todo lo pierde por imbécil y el que nada
tiene y todo lo gana por su esfuerzo, opto por este último.'[1]

Even within 'Adelfos', however, Machado transcended fashion.
In the third stanza of that poem, for example, he got over that
decadent aestheticism (which was indeed susceptible to a charge
of escapism) to allow the possibilities of a real profundity: these
possibilities are fully exploited in 'Eleusis' and 'Lirio' and occur
thematically ('una flor que nace en tierras ignoradas') throughout
his work, from his earliest to his latest period. A useful way of
approaching this theme is to compare 'Lirio' with 'Gerineldos,
el paje', two poems with the same subject but differently developed. For either poem to be successful the reader must be able to
sympathize with Gerineldos's predicament. In the second poem
Machado makes this difficult by using the soulfully fragile phrase
'pobre pajecillo' to describe his subject, and by a coarse insinua-
tion of the queen's invitation to voluptuousness:

> la reina lo ha visto.
> De sedas cubierto,
> sin armas al cinto,
> con alma de nardo,
> con talle de lirio...

[1] See my article 'Antonio Machado y Álvarez and Positivism'.

These lines evoke the sickly atmosphere of Villaespesa's 'Neuróticas':

> ¡ Oh, mi alma, mi alma es un lirio,
> es un lirio de amor, todo blanco,
> que al altar de una virgen ofrece
> en sus pálidos dedos un santo ¡ [1]

There is no progress within 'Gerineldos, el paje'. The solace offered to the 'alma' of Gerineldos and therefore of the reader is less sublime than sensual. The queen and her lover may be decadent and exquisite, but they are still sexual symbols and the garden of their loves is limited and confined, as in the original ballad Machado read in Agustín Durán's *Romancero*:

> ¿Dónde vas buen Gerineldos?
> ¿Cómo estás tan sin sentido?
> —Paseaba por estos jardines
> para ver si han florecido
> y ví que una fresca rosa
> el calor ha deslucido. [2]

Gerineldos is addressed by the King after his furtive love-making. Charlemagne's prurient daughter Emma has become a queen and the gallant Eginard a pallid page boy, but the sequence of events is preserved and the lovers are still lovers in the crudest sense.

Some of the distinctive features of Machado's second and better poem 'Lirio' can, however, be found still within the *Romancero*. Durán appended to the ballad a shorter *corrío* or *carrerilla* which, like 'Lirio', has two, not three, characters, is no longer subject to a time sequence and in which great emphasis is laid on Gerineldos's restless wandering:

> ¿Dónde vienes Gerineldos
> tan triste y tan afligido?
> —Vengo del jardín, señora,
> de coger flores y lirios. [3]

In these opening lines Gerineldos's malaise is no longer just sexual; he is more like Teodoro in the third act of Lope's *El perro del hortelano*, a play Machado knew as a child and which he claimed

---

[1] *La copa*, p. 67.
[2] 1851 edition, I, p. 176. (No. 321), cf. p.126 below. [3] *Ibid.*

'me ha llegado muy adentro'.[1] Teodoro spoke for Gerineldos
when he answered Tristán's question:

> Señor, ¿adónde vas?
> Lo mismo ignoro
> porque de suerte estoy, Tristán amigo,
> que no sé donde voy ni quien me lleva.
> Solo y sin alma, el pensamiento sigo.[2]

Later in the same act Teodoro addresses his queen in a phrase of
arresting lyricism memorable and distinct from the rest of the
scene:

> Señora, vuelvo por mí
> que no estoy en otra parte.
> Y como me he de llevar,
> vengo para que me des
> a mi mismo.[3]

In 'Lirio', Gerineldos, breaking out of the cloying garden, searches
in the same way for rest and his own image:

> Como una humareda,
> como un pensamiento...
> como esa persona
> extraña, que vemos
> cruzar por las calles
> oscuras de un sueño.

His state of mind is the same as Machado's in that third stanza of
'Adelfos', different in structure (with its unorthodox alexandrines)
and tone from the rest of the poem:

> En mi alma, hermana de la tarde, no hay contornos,
> ...y la rosa simbólica de mi única pasión
> es una flor que nace en tierras ignoradas
> y que no tiene aroma, ni forma, ni color.

This trance-like state of a man intoxicated by the scentless
oleanders, and who looks for beauty and peace in a remote land,
was dramatized by Machado in 'Eleusis' and, indirectly, that
peace was identified with death. Those who made the pilgrimage
to Eleusis every September to worship at Ceres's shrine went not

[1] M. J. Moya, 'Preguntas de *El Alcázar*'. He also translated the play—see the
Bibliography.   [2] Kohler's edition, Paris, 1934, I, 2518–23.   [3] *Ibid.* 2645–9.

to gain knowledge, but to be comforted and feel the power of their goddess, παθεῖν καὶ διατεθηναί. They believed that death was not an evil but a blessing. Machado followed the elusive, golden-haired goddess, the equivalent of Gerineldos's queen, in a trance-like state:

> Se perdió en las vagas
> selvas de un ensueño,
> y sólo de espaldas
> la vi desde lejos...
> Como una caricia
> dorada, el cabello,
> tendido, sus hombros
> cubría. Y al verlo,
> siguióla mi alma
> y fuése muy lejos,
> dejándome solo,
> no sé si dormido o despierto.

E. Gómez de Baquero said of 'Eleusis' and 'Adelfos': 'son de lo más penetrante que ha producido la lírica contemporánea española'.[1] Machado's treatment of this theme of the subconscious association of love and death in *Alma* is certainly suggestive and closely knit. Yet it is interesting to see its fortune at other stages in his work.[2] In an adolescent poem 'Antes' he showed himself already attracted by the sleep-giving oleander, but in an admittedly trivial way:

> sólo quiero
> ya, las adormideras sin olores
> que sólo dan, agradecidas, sueño.

After its elaboration in *Alma* the theme suffered a number of crude interpretations in *Caprichos* and *Alma. Museo. Los Cantares*, before reappearing in *Ars moriendi* in poems like the shallow 'Morir, dormir...':

> — Hijo, para descansar
> es necesario dormir,
> no pensar,
> no sentir,
> no soñar...
> — Madre, para descansar,
> morir.

[1] 'El *Ars moriendi* de Manuel Machado.'
[2] The theme of the play *Las adelfas* is different despite its title.

Another poem on the same theme in *Ars moriendi* is far more subtle:

> Morir es...Una flor hay en el sueño
> — que al despertar no está ya en nuestras manos—
> de aromas y colores imposibles...
> Y un día sin aurora la cortamos.

Here death is sleep, the 'adelfa', but it is also something else. Dawn may be the vanishing of the flower, but having awoken the poet can always repossess the flower again in sleep. On the dawnless day of death possession of the flower is complete, but the flower is plucked at last and unrepeatably. This brief poem is Machado's most intricate and beautiful statement of the theme: the spikenard soul, in the thrall of an impossible queen, is presented with the chill paradox of the fulfilment of its desire. Towards the end of his life Machado resolved this paradox in his religious poetry: his desire was given a surer object; Mary's arms, kinder than those of Ceres or Gerineldos's queen, shielded him from the abyss of nothingness and promised an eternal replucking of the flower.

The paradox so neatly stated in that quatrain from *Ars moriendi* was already inherent in *Alma* if not, as later, within any one poem. In other poems in the section 'El reino interior', especially 'Los días sin sol' and 'El jardín gris', Machado expressed what was at that time in Spain a modern notion of existentialism; even if he felt himself dragged on to Eleusis, ultimately he had no illusions about what he would find on arriving. In this Manuel Machado was less sentimental than many of his contemporaries. His treatment of the 'parque viejo' theme has been shown to differ radically from that of his brother or Juan Ramón Jiménez.[1] Eyes cannot look along the white paths of Manuel Machado's garden, not because they are filled with tears, but because they cannot visualize nothingness. Machado was writing about the irrelevance of sentimentality in the face of non-existence:

> ¡Tu soledad es tanta
> que no deja poesía a tu tristeza![2]
> ¡Llegando a ti se muere la mirada!
> Cementerio sin tumbas...

[1] See p. 105 above.
[2] Cf. again Antonio Machado: 'tierras...tan tristes que tienen alma' ('La tierra de Alvargonzález').

Ni una voz, ni recuerdos ni esperanza.
Jardín sin jardinero,
viejo jardín,
        viejo jardín sin alma.   ('El jardín gris')

This idea of the white silence of nothingness occurs again in the bitterly frivolous 'Pantomima', where what is left of an absurd life slowly vanishes into the stillness of a fresh snowfall:

Muere al fin la última risa
sin que el viento se la lleve...
Cae la nieve,
y está la tierra en camisa...
¿Por qué no ríe Margot?...[1]

It occurs yet again in 'Los días sin sol' where the white wolf of winter threatens all with annihilation and oblivion.

El lobo blanco del invierno,
el lobo blanco viene.

This poem is unique in Machado's work: still responding at a deep emotional level and without any facile preaching he is nevertheless less of a nihilist. Unamuno was right to see a connection between 'Los días sin sol' and Leopardi's 'La ginestra', the symbol of life in the desolation of a petrified lava flow.[2] By means of a series of uninsistent exclamations Machado creates an idea of a human solidarity out of the irrational security man feels when turning in on himself and sheltering from a hostile universe, out of the intimacy which allows the frivolity of '¡Dios no nos quiere!':

¡Reunámonos, que todos
tengan una familia,
un libro y un fuego alegre!

Y mientras, fuera, el hacha
el tronco seco hiende,
que será rojo en el hogar, cerremos
la puerta y el balcón... ¡Dios no nos quiere!

---

[1] Throughout the poem a deathly white (Pierrot's face, the moon, etc.) gradually encroaches on the gaiety of the pantomime and stifles it. However these 'personajes terriblemente tristes', as Dámaso Alonso called them, are too near to caricature for notions of colour symbolism to be taken more seriously here.

[2] Prologue to *Alma. Museo. Los Cantares*, p. xv.

¡Tregua! Seamos amigos...
La tibia paz entre nosotros reine,
en torno de la lámpara que esparce
la tranquila poesía del presente.

Darío had used similar images in 'Invernal': the lamp, the fire
inside; the cold outside:

De la apacible estancia
en la extensión tranquila
vertería la lámpara reflejos
de luces opalinas
Dentro, amor que abrasa;
fuera, la noche fría;[1]

But the hostile winter prompted in him not a desire for solidarity
but erotic fantasy:

Los lechos abrigados,
las almohadas mullidas,
las pieles de Astracán, los besos cálidos
que dan las bocas húmedas y tibias.[2]

Machado's poem is his most generous interpretation of 'la vida
interior, que preside la lámpara, amiga íntima'. It is the poetic
version of a vision he described in more detail in a short story of
the time, of man in his 'pequeño mundo primitivo': 'El padre que
distribuye pan rodeado de los hijos y la madre que alimenta el
hogar. La primera sociedad, apenas emancipada de la caverna,
todavía tiranizada por el lobo que aulla de frío y de hambre en
torno a la choza. Hé aquí todo—todo.'[3]

In certain poems in *Alma*, Manuel Machado concerned himself
with his subconscious. His method of expression was often
deceptively uninsistent and people who read those poems superficially fail to see their interconnection and deny Machado depth.
This opinion is typical of many: 'Su lirismo no nace de una vida
interior intensa...sino de estímulos externos.'[4] However, at his
best he penetrated further into his 'reino interior' than most of his
contemporaries and produced poems that are important for a
proper understanding not only of his own work but of a period
of Spanish poetry. It is only unfortunate that he failed almost
completely to develop the gifts he displayed in *Alma*.

[1] *Azul...*   [2] *Ibid.*   [3] 'La convalecencia', *El amor*, p. 64.
[4] Angel del Río, *Historia de la literatura española* (New York, 1948), ii, p. 211.

11

'MUSEO'
(PHILIP IV AND CHARLES V)

> L'image au sépulcre ravie
> perd son aspect roide et glacé;
> la chaude pourpre de la vie
> remonte aux veines du passé.
> —Théophile Gautier, 'Le Château du souvenir'

'Nadie más cortesano ni púlido que nuestro rey Felipe, que Dios guarde.'[1] This phrase, with the conversational 'que Dios guarde', could have been uttered in good faith by a seventeenth-century courtier about a monarch appropriately more courtly and courteous than any of his subjects. To the regenerationists of the beginning of this century on the other hand, possession of such qualities seemed less than kingly and praise of them untoward. Machado, like Velázquez, did not preclude either attitude. 'Felipe IV' is an accomplished example of what Machado set out to achieve in his 'portrait' poems: 'He procurado la síntesis de los sentimientos de la época y del pintor; la significación y el estado del arte en todo tiempo; la evocación del espíritu de los tiempos; la sensación producida hoy en nosotros.'[2] The possibilities of multiple interpretation offered in the opening lines are maintained throughout the poem.

> Es pálida su tez como la tarde,
> cansado el oro de su pelo undoso,
> y de sus ojos, el azul, cobarde.

In this second tercet, the vivid description of a certain physical type, the verbal equivalent of Velázquez's brush strokes, could also be a comment on an age: the face pale like the evening of the day when the sun never set, and as empty of life-blood as a declining

---

[1] 'Felipe IV.'   [2] *La Guerra Literaria*, p. 44.

Spain; the golden hair lustreless and weak like the supply of gold from America.

> Sobre su augusto pecho generoso
> ni joyeles perturban ni cadenas
> el negro terciopelo silencioso.

It would be difficult to praise the last line of the third tercet more highly than Dámaso Alonso has done:

El negro terciopelo silencioso! Habría en las palabras una inmovibilidad de densa materia quieta si la intercalación del sustantivo entre los dos adjetivos no diera reprimida fluencia de paño sin rumor. Es, sin duda, el verso más expresivo que ha salido de la pluma de Manuel Machado, uno de los mayores aciertos de la poesía española contemporánea.[1]

The power of the line could again be explained in terms of the same ambiguity: the velvet, black and silent in the museum, expressing the utter remoteness and sadness of past glory and then, paradoxically, the king in that tangible velvet regaining the fluidity and the immediacy of life. Lines like this one give Machado's phrase 'en Velázquez veo la vida' a precise meaning.

> Y, en vez de cetro real, sostiene apenas
> con desmayo galán, un guante de ante
> la blanca mano de azuladas venas.

This last tercet lightens the darkness of the previous one and carefully echoes the ambiguity of the first tercet. The king is on the one hand reprehensibly decadent, forgetting the royal sceptre for a suede glove; on the other hand he is delightfully so, with his poise, his refinement and his blue-veined hands. This last detail was designed to appeal particularly and directly to the aristocratic taste of the Modernists in an anaemic mood. In none of Velázquez's known portraits of Philip IV, and certainly in none in the Prado, the Museo de Madrid and the Louvre, the art galleries Machado knew well, does the king actually hold a suede glove; a book, a scroll, yes, but not a glove. Machado was introducing this detail to some purpose, taking the liberty he confessed to taking with the original paintings in his portrait poems: 'teniendo muy bien cuidado de cometer ciertas inexactitudes que son del todo necesarias a mi intento'.[2] The glove sharpens our focus on the regal

---

[1] 'Ligereza y gravedad', p. 96.   [2] *La Guerra Literaria*, p. 44.

hand: those aristocratic hands Darío claimed for himself ('mis manos de marqués') and which Valle-Inclán evoked in the *Sonata de Otoño* in a phrase startlingly similar to that of Machado's poem: 'las manos blancas que en los viejos retratos sostienen apenas los pañolitos de encaje.'[1] And Machado himself, by pressing his own claim to being a descendant of the Marqués de Montevelo, who renounced his country in order to remain a courtier of Philip IV,[2] showed that he too had a weakness for the aristocratic airs otherwise displayed in 'Adelfos' ('De mi alta aristocracia dudar jamás se pudo', etc.). But in 'Felipe IV' he was not just decadent: he does not criticize, but he does not fawn. The poem in its elusiveness is one of Machado's great achievements. None of the adjectives comprises the ample, subtle tone, yet the atmosphere could not be more precisely detailed.

Machado was the first Spanish poet to devote a poem to a painting, scrupulously following the movement of another art form as he might that of a poem in another language. Before him, no one in Spain, with the interest in the fusion of the arts so typical of the period, had confined his attention exclusively to one picture and found there inspiration for a whole poem. Machado was encouraged to do this by two things: by his education at the *Institución libre de enseñanza*, and by the experiments of the Parnassians and the Spanish American Modernists. One of the distinctive features of the *Institución*'s educational method was the rejection of any prior, rigid but necessarily arbitrary account of history and art, in favour of the attempt to make pupils acquire standards of judgement only through a refinement of direct personal experience. During visits to art galleries and museums (the beginning of a life-long habit with Manuel Machado), Giner de los Ríos and M. B. Cossío would stand impassive before a picture in order not to prejudice their pupils' response; only when

[1] As it first appeared in *Electra* (March 1901), 'Felipe IV' was possibly one of the poems Machado read aloud to the group at Fuencarral. *Sonata de Otoño* is of 1902.

[2] See pp. 44–5 above; in Machado's correspondence in the *BMB* there is a note from the Secretary to the King of Portugal (Lisbon, 23 December 1902) which suggests Machado unsuccessfully tried to gain permission to use a noble title at this period.

it had come would they inform and elaborate, by knowledgeably placing the picture in a school or an age.[1] This experience and this instruction given to Machado were enriched by his familiarity with French poetry, the Parnassians and Verlaine,[2] and with the work of Spanish American Modernists: the Darío of the 'medallones' and, strikingly, Guillermo Valencia and Julián del Casal. Valencia, whom Machado may have known in Paris, published in *Ritos* both a poem on an engraving by Dürer and a sonnet very much in the style of Machado on Hans Holbein's portrait of Erasmus. Casal's *Nieve* (1893) contained a series of ten sonnets, entitled 'Mi museo ideal', on ten paintings by Gustave Moreau; and in the more successful among them, 'Salomé' and 'Galatea' for example, there is a hint of the detailed observation with breadth of response which characterizes Machado's poem. Casal, however, lacked the historical perspective and the sheer erudition which allowed Machado's poetry the possibility of being more than Parnassian mood-setting.

In Spain, where it represented a new idea and a new achievement, 'Felipe IV' attracted many imitators. Juan Ramón Jiménez mentioned them in his essay on Machado: 'Tiene quien le imite escandalosamente haciendo retratos. Pero el óleo de los otros se tuerce pronto, y el de él perdura.'[3] Jiménez may well have been thinking of Antonio de Zayas who wrote a number of 'portrait' poems for the occasion of Alfonso XIII's coming of age in May 1902 and published them later that year under the title *Retratos antiguos*. Zayas's (much less discriminating) attention was also drawn to one of Velázquez's portraits of Philip IV:

> Claros los ojos, pálida la frente,
> el oro del cabello desteñido,
> claro el rubio bigote retorcido,
> grueso el labio, la barba prominente,
>
> correr Felipe por las venas siente
> la noble sangre azul de su apellido,
> de terciopelo negro revestido
> y al cuello el timbre borgoñón pendiente.

---

[1] See my article 'Manuel Machado y la pintura'; the section 'Museo' (which contains 'Felipe IV') in *Alma* was dedicated 'al admirable maestro Giner de los Ríos'.
[2] For his 'César Borgia', see p. 98 above.   [3] 'Alma y Capricho', p. 44.

Oculta el traje que severo luce
de amor y gloria el devorante fuego
que de sus noches el placer inquieta;
y a través de su risa se trasluce
que el Rey sofoca y tapa el palaciego
sus ensueños de amante y de poeta.

Machado does not seem to have resented Zayas's imitating him, perhaps because the competition he offered was so slight; in any case Machado dedicated his 'Felipe IV' to Zayas in *Alma* when, since they were such close friends, he must have known that Zayas was imitating him. And if Machado was the first to write a poem on Philip IV, Zayas anticipated him in composing sonnets on Titian's 'Carlos V', Goya's 'Carlos IV' and 'La reina María Luisa', and on 'La Gioconda', and with his description of Charles IV as 'bonachón' and the farthingale as 'pomposo' he even supplied Machado with useful vocabulary.[1]

In the context of Machado's own work, 'Felipe IV' was the first and the best of a series of its type, although it was not a sonnet,[2] unlike most of his poems on paintings, which were collected in *Apolo* (1911). This book contained more portraits from Philip IV's court, about which he and his brother elsewhere showed detailed historical knowledge in the play *Julianillo Valcárcel*. 'La infanta Margarita', Philip IV's daughter, has many of the characteristics of her father. Machado indicated that again in this sonnet he had tried to capture and not to judge 'toda la elegancia, toda la decadencia, toda la infinita amargura de la deliciosa Infanta'.[3] How her hands resemble her father's:

La mano—ámbar de ensueño—entre los tules
de la falda desmáyase y sostiene
el pañuelo riquísimo.

---

[1] See *Retratos antiguos* (Madrid, 1902), pp. 39, 133, 134 and 30 respectively; and Machado's poems of the titles quoted.

[2] Moreno Villa described 'Felipe IV' as 'versos que ya querían ser soneto' ('La Manolería', p. 121). 'La Venus del hogar', on a study by the Alsatian artist Henner, was first published like most of the sonnets in *Apolo* in 1910, but was excluded from the collection probably because it was not in sonnet form, and because in this poem, as in 'Figulinas', the poem about a princess by Watteau, he was not primarily concerned with the historical and social background which informed the picture.   [3] *La Guerra Literaria*, p. 56.

And how similarly she combines dignity, elegance and fragility:

> Y corona no más su augusta frente
> la dorada ceniza del cabello,
> que apenas prende el leve lazo rosa.

Velázquez's visual effects are again cleverly suggested by Machado in this later poem; he alerts us to the fact that the princess, caught in the complexity of decadence, had had her cheeks painted twice, once with make-up and then by Velázquez:

> el semblante,
> que hábil pincel tiñó de leche y fresa,
> emerge del pomposo guardainfante,
> entre sus galas cortesanas presa.

However, in its greater explicitness, the poem lacks many of the possibilities of its model 'Felipe IV'. For while in 'Felipe IV' Machado said that the king's face was 'pálida como la tarde' merely hinting that 'la tarde' was also the end of the Spanish Empire, his description of the Infanta's face was more direct, forced and therefore limited:

> Italia, Flandes, Portugal...Poniente
> sol de la gloria, el último destello
> en sus mejillas infantiles posa...

Despite Machado's desire to capture 'toda la infinita amargura de la deliciosa Infanta', the statement of the thesis of decadence interrupts the evocation of human presence. Correspondingly, the subject of the poem moves away from character into caricature. 'Don Juan de Austria', Philip IV's buffoon, the deformed inheritor of a glorious name, is aptly caricatured, but also in this sense of being limited, in a third sonnet on Philip IV's court:

> No fue en Lepanto, pese a su alto nombre.
> Pero, amigo de un rey de glorias harto,
> entre sus timbres de alta prez hay uno
> que hace de él un amable gentilhombre:
> prestó un doblón al gran Felipe cuarto
> en cierta noche de terrible ayuno.

The sonnet ends almost like an anecdote, a joke. And for its effect the joke depends on a preconceived theory of that period of history. It is an intelligent comment, an able clothing with words of a fixed idea. If the king in 'Felipe IV' invites speculation and even closer scrutiny, in 'Don Juan de Austria' he is a cardboard figure.

Although in many respects a remarkable poem, 'Carlos V' also depends closely on a theory of history, but of course as a representative of a different period. Philip IV's court represents decadence as Charles V's represents forceful magnificence. Machado was on dangerous ground as he elevated his hero higher on to the dais of a superman:

> lanza en mano,
> recorre su dominio, el Mundo entero,
> con resonantes pasos, y seguros. ('Carlos V')

But then, putting the frame back on the picture, he stepped back to save himself and the poem:

> En este punto lo pintó el Tiziano.

In the poems of this type which Machado wrote after *Apolo*, the tendency to over-simplify, to play with an idea at the expense of human individuality, is even more strongly marked. In a sonnet published in 1938, Charles V was presented simply and straightforwardly as the 'Emperador del Universo entero'. And 'este hombre gris' of *Apolo* became the superlative example of force and austerity of whom Machado wrote twenty-five years later:

> El no tenía que ostentar grandeza
> ni fiar a oropeles el respeto...
> A él le bastaba ser dueño del Mundo.
> ('La litera de Carlos V')

Once he had formed the mould, Machado did little more than fit in the appropriate name before stamping out the sonnets he wrote in praise of the Civil War heroes and military figures. For example, Charles V's 'carnoso labio socarrón, y duros ojos de lobo audaz' were remodelled only slightly for Franco to be better able to 'vencer y sonreír'; and following the Emperor's 'resonantes pasos y seguros' the Generalísimo

> campa en la guerrera gloria
> seguro y firme. ('Francisco Franco')

While the themes of Charles V's grandeur and Philip IV's decadence may have limited Machado's poetic expression, they were
still broad enough for the sonnets of *Apolo* to be plausible. But
the ideas Machado had to clothe with words during the Civil War
deprived his poetry of even that quality. What is remarkable is
that he should have integrated into his sonnets as successfully as he
did the blatant slogans of war-time propaganda, in poems like
'¡Pilarica!', '¡España!' and '¡Emilio Mola! ¡Presente!'.

The difference between Machado's first evocation of Velázquez's
Philip IV and his sketch of the public image of Franco is great.
Yet the tendency from one towards the other is consistent in his
work. And so the circumstances which inclined him to become a
propagandist are, from a literary point of view, secondary. That
approach to poetry, that interested simplification, was nothing
new in his verse. One of the most startlingly improbable of his
descriptions of Franco's Spain had an exact precedent in an earlier
poem.

> ¡España! ¡España!, en el crisol fundida
> de ocho siglos guerreros;
> bastión de Europa en ellos defendida
> de la oriental barbarie y de los fieros africanos.   ('Covadonga')

These lines from a poem written for *La Fiesta de la Raza* in 1921
became—*mutatis mutandis* because of the presence of 'fieros
africanos' in Franco's armies —

> ¡Oh!, la España de Franco, baluarte
> contra la plaga asiática en Europa,
> ¡siempre vocada a la tremenda hazaña!   ('¡España!')

This concept of Spain's role in Europe and the world was already
personified for Machado in Charles V, less crudely perhaps, but
plainly enough, in his sonnet on Titian's portrait. On the other
hand nothing suggests that Machado ever meant Philip IV, in the
first and best portrait poem, to be the symbol of despicable
decadence he was made into by the cult of regeneration and
military prowess which has afflicted Europe so variously and
deeply throughout this century.

12

'LOS CANTARES'

Namen und Nachrichten der Fabel oder Wahrheit zeugen, was damals Poesie war, woraus sie entsprang, worin sie lebte. Sie lebte im Ohr des Volks, auf den Lippen und der Harfe lebendiger Sänger: sie sang Geschichte, Begebenheit, Geheimnis, Wunder und Zeichen: sie war die Blume der Eigenheit eines Volks, seiner Sprache und seines Landes, seiner Geschäfte und Vorurteile, seiner Leidenschaften und Anmaßungen, seiner Musik und Seele.
—J. G. Herder, *Stimmen der Völker in Liedern*

Manuel Machado's *cantares*, poems inspired by traditional, chiefly Andalusian, folk poetry, are a large and important part of his total work. They form a continuous thread stretching from the ballads and *coplas* of *Tristes y Alegres* to poems like 'Sentimiento' published in the *A.B.C.* just before his death. This preponderance and this continuity have earned for him in the eyes of many the title of 'el poeta de los cantares', the role in which he is still most widely known today.

But unfortunately the attention Machado has attracted as a 'popular' poet has rarely assumed the shape of serious criticism. The various motives and qualities of his interest in folk poetry have seldom been distinguished or situated historically. For example, the commonplace contrast between his 'aristocratic' Modernism and his 'popular' Andalusianism is more apparent than real. The admiration Machado expressed for the 'natural spontaneity' of folk poetry, in the prologue to *Cante hondo*[1] and elsewhere, has the same Romantic root that his Modernism has. Indeed, only when this is realized does the pattern of his development as a 'popular' poet begin to emerge. Before his Modernist period he was content to follow the Spanish Romantics in their narrative rather than lyrical use of the ballad, as 'El rescate', an adolescent imitation of Zorrilla in *Triste y Alegres*, shows; in *Alma*, more

[1] 'Las coplas se cantan y se sienten...nacen del corazón, no de la inteligencia. Son gritos no palabras'.

125

in tune with Bécquer and the European Romantics, he explored altogether new depths with 'Lirio' and 'Mariposa negra'.[1] Later in life the nature of his interest in folk poetry was complicated yet again. Political pressures made his use of the word 'popular' still more uncertain, in books like *Cante hondo* and *Sevilla y otros poemas*, and in what he wrote after 1936. In short, Machado's rôle as a popular poet was not a simple one. Such significance as he had in it is closely bound to the social and literary context to which he belonged.

When asked why he first became interested in 'poesía popular', Machado would remind his interrogator that he was related to Agustín Durán and that his father had founded the first folk-lore society in Spain.[2] Machado's home background doubtless fostered his interest; the effect of Cipriana Álvarez Durán's reading her uncle's *Romancero* to him as a child is apparent enough in 'Lirio'. As for Machado y Álvarez himself, it is true that he influenced Manuel Machado, though ultimately this influence provoked a direct reaction.

In the first place, Machado y Álvarez helped his son by making a wealth of traditional *pregones de flores, serranas, soleares* and *coplas* of all types immediately accessible to him, or in some cases by providing a written record of what Manuel himself had heard sung in the streets of Seville as a child and an undergraduate. A few examples will suffice to show how closely Manuel echoed *coplas* collected by his father.

> Las que se publican
> no son grandes penas.
> Las que se callan y se llevan dentro
> son las verdaderas. ('Seguiriyas gitanas')

---

[1] See p. 111 above.

[2] *El Alcázar*, 21 January 1947. This genealogical fact has been adduced almost universally by critics as a single 'explanation' for Machado's 'popular' poetry. D. Alonso was of the opinion that 'la aptitud le venía, sin duda, de casta' ('Ligereza y gravedad'), and A. F. G. Bell thought that 'los cantares...proved his inherited susceptibility to the popular poetry of his native land' (*Contemporary Spanish Literature*, London, 1926, p. 208). See also J. Chabás, *Vuelo y estilo*, p. 97; J. Sampelayo, 'Una hora con M.M.'; J. M. Pemán, 'Don Manuel Machado'; and A. González-Climent, *Antología*, p. 42; and many others.

This *copla*, which he wrote at twenty, has an obvious precedent in one collected by his father:

> No ama mucho quien lo dice,
> sino quien mucho padece;
> que amor sin penas y obras,
> de amor sólo el nombre tiene.[1]

And this one

> Compañerita del alma,
> ¡qué penita pasa aquel
> que tiene el agua en los labios
> y no la puede beber![2]

was a model for Manuel's *soleariya*

> Esta agüita fresca...
> ¡Cómo la tengo en los propios labios
> y no puedo beberla!

Again:

> Cuando te encuentro en la calle
> el sentido me se quita
> y me agarro a las paredes,
> hasta perderte de vista.[3]

anticipated

> Yo me agarro a las paredes
> cuando te encuentro en la calle,
> chiquilla, pa no caerme.   ('Soleares')

Examples of this sort could be multiplied. Machado can be shown to have imitated *coplas* collected by his father and also to have attempted to capture the force of a peculiarly Andalusian topic which his father had drawn attention to. Machado y Álvarez selected, for instance, the following *copla* and remarked on its 'delicadeza y vigor':

> Por dondequiera que voy
> parece que te voy viendo;
> son las sombras del querer
> que me vienen persiguiendo.[4]

---

[1] *Cantes flamencos* (Buenos Aires, Austral), 1947, p. 143; where possible I use this edition for the sake of convenience but employ the regular orthography of the original editions: *Colección de cantes flamencos recogidos y anotados por Demófilo* (Seville, El Porvenir, 1881), xviii and pp. 209, and *Cantes flamencos; colección escogida*, Madrid, Tomás Rey, 1889, pp. 232. See also his *Biblioteca de tradiciones populares españolas*, vol. v (Seville, 1884) (= *BTPE*).

[2] *Ibid.* p. 78.   [3] *Ibid.* p. 78.

[4] *Ibid.* p. 59; for Machado y Álvarez's commentary see *BTPE*, v, 30.

His son caught something of this power in

> ¿De qué me sirve dejarte
> si dondequiera que miro
> te me pones por delante?　　　　　　('Soleares')

Again two of Machado's *coplas* rely on the Andalusian idea of a woman being 'sembrá' ('graceful', 'beautiful'):

> El andar de mi morena
> parece que va sembrando
> lirios, palmas y azucenas.　　　　　　(*Ibid.*)

and

> Rosita y mosquetas,
> claveles y nardos
> en sus andares, la mi compañera
> los va derramando.　　　　　('Seguiriyas gitanas')

Machado y Álvarez had already drawn attention to the originality of this idea in his commentary on the traditional *solear*:

> Esa mujer está sembrá;
> va derramando mosquetas
> por dondequiera que va.[1]

These parallels between the traditional poetry collected and discussed by Machado y Álvarez and that which Manuel wrote in traditional forms are illuminating, and prove a degree of indebtedness. However, Machado y Álvarez's influence went still deeper. He also helped Manuel Machado to create the little original poetry he wrote in this genre, that is, poetry which was no longer confined to the limits of traditional forms. 'La pena' and 'El querer', are two of the poems most interesting in this respect. As a lawyer in the early 1870s, Machado y Álvarez came across a case of acute poisoning in an Andalusian village. On questioning the victim, a stone-mason, he learnt that the man had been given the lethal potion by a girl who claimed to be deeply in love with him. She had given her lover the drink believing in a folk superstition according to which she could bind him to her ('ligarlo'), make him desire only her, once he had drunk a certain mixture of herbs. So Machado y Álvarez argued that the following *copla*

---

[1] *Cantes flamencos*, p. 35.

was not just metaphorical but had an immediate meaning in the context of Andalusian folk-lore:

> Yo no sé por dónde,
> ni por dónde no,
> se me ha liao esta soguita al cuerpo
> sin saberlo yo.[1]

Manuel Machado picked out this *copla* and put it as a final stanza to 'La pena'. In turn, the power of the images of his poem owes something to the folkloric background his father had explored. 'La pena', the poison spreading its roots through the chest like ivy, bitter but given to consummate a passion:

> Mi pena es muy mala,
> porque es una pena que yo no quisiera
> que se me quitara.
>
> Vino y se ha quedado
> en mi corazón,
> como el amargo en la corteza verde
> del verde limón.
>
> Como las raíces
> de la enredadera
> se va alimentando la pena en mi pecho
> con sangre *e* mis venas.

The same idea of an obsessive painful passion, satisfied only with utter possession and death, underlies the more successful stanzas of 'El querer':

> Yo quisiera ser el aire
> que toda entera te abraza;
> yo quisiera ser la sangre
> que corre por tus entrañas.
>
> Siento al ceñir tu cintura
> una duda que me mata,
> que quisiera en un abrazo
> todo tu cuerpo y tu alma.
>
> Estoy enfermo de ti,
> de curar no hay esperanza,
> que, en la sed de este amor loco,
> tú eres mi sed y mi agua.

[1] *Cantes flamencos* (Seville, 1881), pp. 98–9.

Machado's expression of this feeling was further helped by another *copla* collected by his father:

> Quisiera ser el sepulcro
> donde a tí te han de enterrar,
> para tenerte en mis brazos
> por toda la eternidad.[1]

Examples of this sort of influence could again be multiplied. The 'cambio', and the syncopated rhythms of Andalusian *coplas*, both, as Moreno Villa has shown,[2] important features of Machado's poetry, were amply studied by Machado y Álvarez. 'Cantaora', a sweeping review of the singers of *cante hondo*, is the poetic version of Machado y Álvarez's careful notes. More generally, Machado's attention was in all probability first drawn to the world of *cante hondo* and the gypsy by his father. As an undergraduate, Manuel may have listened to *cantaores* in the tradition of those singers he named: El Fillo, Silverio, Curro Dulce and La Lola herself, but as a creative poet he also inherited all his father had discovered about the gypsy tradition, the 'misterioso y desconocido pueblo gitano' who sang in 'harmonías desconocidas para nosotros'.[3] The appeal of the medieval 'musica ficta' and its descendant *flamenco*, with its quarter tones and resolutions to the dominant and not the tonic, is in some respects similar to that of jazz, an equally primitive music, with its insistence on unresolved dominant sevenths. Machado expressed something of this appeal in 'Cantares': 'algo que caricia', anticipation is aroused; 'algo que desgarra', then it is cheated, and 'la pena', unfulfilled desire, more cruelly felt.

Estimates of Manuel Machado's achievements as an Andalusian poet vary considerably. Gerardo Diego, Juan Chabás, Dámaso Alonso, Andrés González-Climent and many others share Moreno Villa's opinion: 'Los cantares no habían sido desdeñados por los poetas del XIX, especialmente los del litoral. Pero en los de Manolo hubo una más pura e íntima fusión con lo verdaderamente gitano o flamenco; una mayor inteligencia de lo genuina-

---

[1] *Cantes flamencos* (1947), p. 151. This idea was echoed again in 'Musica di camera. III'.
[2] 'La Manolería y el cambio.'   [3] *BTPE*, v, pp. 94–100.

mente "cañí". Machado hizo lo que en la música hicieron Albéniz y Falla':[1]

> Madre, pena, suerte, pena, madre, muerte,
> ojos negros, negros, y negra la suerte...
> cantares...
> En ellos el alma del alma se vierte.

('Cantares')

More specifically Moreno Villa saw Machado as the link between nineteenth-century folk-lore and the world of Lorca and Alberti: 'Yo no creo que sin Manolo Machado hubieran conseguido García Lorca y Alberti la desenvoltura y la emoción gitana que consiguieron. A una gran parte de los poetas andaluces nos sirvió de estímulo.'[2] On the other hand, Lorca is just as often thought to have created his world without the slightest help from Machado, who is dismissed as a servile *coplero*. Flys, writing of Lorca's *Cante Jondo*, leaves no doubt on this point: '...exprime la pura esencia del canto andaluz en su interpretación poética. No se trata de la imitación popular al estilo de Manuel Machado.'[3] Among others, Cejador Frauca and Luis Cernuda also insisted that Machado was not at all original: 'El cante hondo de Manuel Machado es...una mera reproducción no siempre feliz del caudal poético popular.'[4] Indeed a very large proportion of Machado's Andalusian poetry is restricted to the limits of the traditional forms. His *seguidillas gitanas* have, regularly, four lines of 7.5. (7 & 4). 7 or 6.6.10.6. syllables, assonanced abcb; his *soleares* three lines 8.8.8, aba; his *malagueñas* four lines 8.8.8.8, abcb, and so on. Types range from the pure *cante hondo*, 'el cante grande', of the *siguiriya* and the *solear*, whose origin is obscure, to 'el cante chico' or flamenco of the *sevillana, fandango, chufla, alegría* and so on, despised by the older *cantaores* as a degenerate innovation.[5] A statistical analysis of

---

[1] 'La Manolería y el cambio', p. 104. For the other critics mentioned see respectively: *A.B.C.*, 11 December 1947; *Vuelo y estilo*, p. 109; 'Ligereza y gravedad', p. 78: and *Antología*, p. 41.   [2] *Ibid.* p. 125.

[3] *El lenguaje poético de Federico García Lorca* (Madrid, 1955), p. 36.

[4] *Historia de la literatura española* (Madrid, 1920), XII, p. 60; Cernuda is quoted by González-Climent, *Antología*, p. 41.

[5] For more detailed information on the metrics of *cante hondo* see E. Torner, 'La canción tradicional española', *Carreras y Candi* (Barcelona, 1934), II, pp. 7–61 and T. Navarro, *Métrica española* (New York, 1956), pp. 447–55.

Machado's *cantares* reveals an early preference for the former. Before 1907 he had written 60% of his *seguidillas* and 22% of his *soleares*, but only 9% of his *alegrías* and *sevillanas*. There is a detectable corresponding decline in quality: homely wisdom, maudlin religiosity and sensual 'ayes' tend to increase at the expense of poignancy and subtlety. But for all 'la emoción gitana' he may have expressed at any period, Machado cannot reasonably be said to have influenced anyone directly when writing *coplas* in the traditional mould.[1] Lorca and Alberti could just as easily have gone straight back to the traditional *coplas* collected by Machado y Álvarez or any of the numerous folklorists of the late nineteenth and early twentieth century, if they did not actually collect them themselves. Besides, Machado was not alone in imitating *coplas*; the poets he mentioned in his prologue to *Cante hondo*, Ferrán, Trueba, Montoto, Trovas and Paradas, preceded him, and so did a host of others whose work was published in a plethora of paper-backed anthologies early this century.

If Machado influenced later poets it was as a writer of original poetry, of poems like 'Cantares', 'La pena' and 'El querer' which absorbed traditional poetry and made out of it something new and more compelling. The question of Machado's influence is complicated by the probability that Moreno Villa, who admired Machado and definitely influenced Lorca, was a further link in the chain which stretches from nineteenth-century folk-lore to *El romancero gitano*. Luis Cernuda, who despised Manuel Machado as a poet and a man, attributed great importance to Moreno Villa at Machado's expense.[2] Moreno Villa himself however told a different story. He could not have been more complimentary to Machado when dedicating his *Luchas de 'pena' y 'alegría'* (Madrid, 1915) to him: 'En el atrio de este recogido poema, quiero que, como un fuste pentélico, se destaque el nombre de Manuel

---

[1] Although he was more successful in capturing the essence of the traditional *copla* than, say, Ferrán before him, his imitative talent was his limitation. Except in the cases mentioned already it is not possible to approach Machado in the way Daniel Devoto has approached Lorca. (Cf. 'Notas sobre el elemento tradicional en la obra de García Lorca', *Filología*, II (Buenos Aires, 1950), p. 320.

[2] *Estudios sobre poesía española contemporánea* (Madrid, 1957), p. 155.

Machado. En él vive Andalucía.' In view of the fervour of
Moreno Villa's praise there seems little reason for not accepting
Machado's importance, even if his influence was limited to a
few poems and probably passed to Lorca and Alberti through
Moreno Villa. On the other hand, if Machado's importance is
accepted, it must also be defined. If some have ignored Machado
unjustly, others have exaggerated his role as 'el inaugurador del
tema flamenco'.

The general image of Andalusia, the cities, the sun and the dark-
skinned women, was old in literature long before Machado took
it up and his interpretation of it, except for the special cases mentioned later, hardly differs from that of Salvador Rueda or
Villaespesa. It has been argued that Machado anticipated Lorca,
more particularly in a number of poems about *cante hondo*, about
the music of the guitar and the peculiar character of the *solear*, for
instance. But it is not enough to compare titles which are often
identical; the poems themselves must be examined. Lorca's 'La
guitarra'[1] and Machado's 'La guitarra habla' are useful examples.
Both poems are representative: Machado's of all he wrote on this
theme, with the obvious exception of 'Cantares'; Lorca's of the
first period Machado is supposed to have influenced.

In his poem Machado is outside his subject, despite the personification of the guitar, whose feelings the poet ostensibly makes
his own. It is a coarse personification which clamours for attention
and adds nothing to the development of a complex idea, unlike
Lorca's personification of the *siguiriya*: 'Muchacha morena...
encadenada al temblor de un ritmo que nunca llega.'[2] The distorted syntax (l. 4: 'como en un corazón guardan vibrante') and
the banality of the adjectives (l. 12: 'magníficos raudales') are due
to the exigencies of a full-rhymed sonnet and 'La guitarra habla'
gains no more from this repression than the average national
anthem. Even the device of 'puntos suspensivos', used with dis-
cretion in *Alma*, assumes in this poem the double role of reviving
an exhausted sentence, and of arch-suggestiveness (l. 11: 'arrullo

---

[1] 'Poema de Cante jondo 1921', *Obras Completas*, Buenos Aires, Losada, 1938,
  IV, p. 76. (= *OC*).
[2] *OC*, IV, p. 80.

blando...'). The real betrayal of Manuel Machado, 'sevillano hasta la médula', comes in the second stanza:

> Llovidas entre exóticas canciones
> ....
> son mis notas calientes goterones.

The important word is obviously 'exóticas'. Machado's basic lack of involvement and honesty in his self-stylisation produces imprecision and superficiality. The 'suerte y pena, amor y muerte' of this poem are fuzzy shadows of the clean precision of 'La pena' and 'El querer'.

There is no spurious personification in Lorca's poem; he is more honest and thorough in trying to express the sound of the guitar and what it evokes. The faltering, sinuous verse form, with its syncopated repetition, indicates a finer sense of adaptation to the subject. The two poets' use of the adjective 'caliente' is something of a clue. Machado's 'calientes goterones de sangre roja' epitomize his appeal to superficial sensuality. The image in Lorca's poem, 'arena del Sur caliente que pide camelias blancas' is equally typical of his attitude. 'Blanco' is not the straightforward opposite of 'caliente'; the underlying thought is subtler, of purity, and desire, relief and thirst, delicacy and force. The 'pena' of the cadence resolving into the dominant not the tonic. This is an effect Machado could begin to create only in his best period. What Machado, in 'La guitarra habla', describes opaquely and kills with a cliché ('suerta y pena, amor y muerte') Lorca presents incarnate:

> Llora flecha sin blanco
> la tarde sin mañana
> y el primer pájaro muerto
> sobre la rama.

The difference between Machado's 'Dice la guitarra' and 'Elogio de la solear' on the one hand, and Lorca's 'Las seis cuerdas' and 'La Soleá'[1] on the other, is explicable in similar terms. While the word 'corazón' concludes Lorca's poem powerfully, in 'La guitarra habla' it acquires the tritest overtones. Machado has the air of a competent ringmaster arranging tame concepts, the degenerate equivalent of Lorca's hunter of images. Lorca's guitar

[1] *OC*, iv, p. 104 and p. 89 respectively.

weeps for the distant things of *cante hondo* which had ceased to hold Machado's attention. For chronology is an important factor in Machado's Andalusian poetry. The theme is entirely absent from *Alma* and *Caprichos*, except of course for the remarkable 'Cantares'. The few *cantares* in *Alma. Museo. Los Cantares* are the most ambitious and successful in this genre. In 1912 however Machado brought to light poetry he had previously discarded, the *coplas* of *Tristes y Alegres*, and donned his cape in earnest: 'Yo mismo andaluz, sevillano hasta la médula (de allí soy, de allí mis padres y mis abuelos), canto al estilo de mi tierra los sentimientos propios.'[1] Once he had started, he kept strumming his guitar through *Sevilla y otros poemas* and several editions of *Cante hondo*, yet his talk of 'exotic refrains' showed him to be no longer concerned with the *cante hondo* which had once haunted him and would haunt Lorca.[2]

The two books in which Machado exploited rather than explored 'popular' and Andalusian poetry, *Cante hondo* and *Sevilla y otros poemas*, were financially his most successful. He soon found that verse about the picturesque southern street, the typical Sevillian wife waiting for her manly and absent husband, the sensual *juerga*, the delights of *manzanilla* and so on had a ready market as tourist propaganda and advertising material.[3] In itself this coherent and repellent image of Andalusia was harmless enough. But on occasion Manuel Machado went too far. For instance, in the play *La Lola se va a los puertos* which he wrote with his brother:

> El pueblo es fino, sensible,
> y, a su modo, aristocrático.
> Trabaja como ninguno
> pero lo hace cantando,
> y, más artista que obrero,
> se ufana del resultado.[4]

---

[1] Prologue to *Cante hondo*.
[2] There is even the possibility of influence in the other direction, i.e. of Lorca and Alberti on the Machado of *Phoenix*: the sophisticated reticence and the metrical dexterity of this later volume is distinctly reminiscent of *Marinero en tierra*. However, because there is no concrete example of influence, this point must remain a moot one.
[3] For example: 'La mujer sevillana', 'Velada sevillana', 'La manzanilla'.
[4] Act I, scene 10; while expressing these and similar sentiments José Luis is shown to be a desirable sort of *señorito*.

A fine distinction, which some critics soon obliterated,[1] separates this from the image of the peasant laughing under the lash, treading the sod with dew on the brow, struggling for his 'mantón bordao' and endowed with spiritual not material values and so on. In his role of Andalusian poet, Machado willingly identified himself with the *pueblo*: 'Y en el fondo, yo mismo, cuando hago cantares, soy pueblo por el sentir y el hablar.'[2] Yet his own way of life, his erratic politics and the partial view of the *pueblo* he presented in his poetry suggest that his eagerness to be of the people as a poet was something of a substitute for real engagement. Only as a member of the staff of *La Libertad* did Machado effectively ally himself with the people: precisely during that period he temporarily lost interest in his 'poesía popular'. A literary socialism, without consequences in actual life, prompted him to say, relying on the Romantic creed of the people,

> Procura tú que tus coplas.
> vayan al pueblo a parar,
> aunque dejen de ser tuyas
> para ser de los demás.
>
> Que al fundir el corazón
> en el alma popular,
> lo que se pierde de nombre
> se gana de eternidad.   ('Cualquier canta un cantar...')

With unwitting irony González-Climent said that Machado was always 'señorialmente popular'. Like Miguel Sawa,

> Vivió para la democracia...;
> pero nunca pudo vencer
> de su fatal aristocracia
> el exquisito parecer.
>
> Y aunque estrechó las rudas manos,
> amó y alternó con los pobres,
> y alzó la copa popular...
>
> Nunca tuvo gestos villanos,
> ni se manchó con los cobres,
> ni fue a pedir, ni fue a votar.   ('Miguel Sawa. Epitafio')

As a 'popular' poet Machado helped to forge that odious union of nationalism and uncommitted socialism which has afflicted not

---

[1] Particularly J. M. Pemán in 'La poesía de M.M.'   [2] Prologue to *Cante hondo*.

only Spain in the last fifty years. It is necessary to say this because of the cynical or ingenuous nonsense which has come out of Franco's Spain about Machado's inherited fidelity to the people, about the way Machado, like Bécquer or even Góngora, was the better Spaniard for having gone to the *pueblo* for inspiration. Few words have been more abused than 'popular'. Machado himself, on entering the Real Academia in 1938, found himself obliged to suggest that the essence of the Spanish people was a kind of life-belt which saved him from drowning in foreign obscurity.[1] This sort of idea relies on the confusion the Positivists tried to avoid when they showed that the people did not create art as a body, and, more significantly, that they were in this matter of folk art dependent on social environment and were, as a group, primitive, illiterate and largely agricultural, and therefore incompatible with modern industrial society. To equate such a group with the 'people' in a political or national sense was misguided or disingenuous. As a Krausist, Antonio Machado y Álvarez sympathized with the Romantic attitudes of his great-uncle Augustín Durán and others, but later he came to agree consciously and definitively with the Positivists; he even went so far as to say: 'El pueblo es para mí el nombre con que pomposamente bautizamos una de nuestras ignorancias que sólo la ciencia conseguirá disipar.'[2] Like Menéndez Pidal and other members of their generation, Manuel and Antonio Machado attempted in their various ways to soften the blow; thus their father's influence on them, contrary to common belief, cannot be said to be in any sense direct. Antonio tended towards a more Romantic idea of the *pueblo* in his ambiguous prologue to *Campos de Castilla*,[3] and Manuel just as ambiguously wished his *coplas* to be absorbed into

[1] Referring to his life in Paris he said: 'Y pulsé como nunca la guitarra andaluza, la que tiene en sus lagrimones toda la sal de España'; this gave J. M. Pemán the opportunity to discuss the role of 'Andalucía salvadora' in Machado's 'heredada fidelidad al pueblo' (*Unos versos*, pp. 68 and 138). Pemán also described Machado's escape from 'la absoluta extranjería' and 'la cerrada obscuridad' in 'Don Manuel Machado'.

[2] See my article 'Antonio Machado y Álvarez and Positivism'.

[3] Luis Cernuda expressed surprise at the sentence: 'Mis romances no emanan de las heroicas gestas, sino del pueblo que las compuso' (*Estudios sobre poesía española contemporánea* (Madrid, 1957), p. 110.

the sea of popular poetry in his introduction to *Cante hondo* the same year[1] and in the poems discussed earlier. But it is true that he was for the most part discreet enough not to commit himself in the way he was forced to during and after the Civil War.

As a Modernist, Manuel Machado found elements of primitive poetry pleasing, and successfully integrated them into his poetry. At its best his Andalusian poetry was original and prepared the way for the poets who came after him. But he exaggerated a tendency when he posed as a spontaneous, 'popular' poet, and on occasion gave himself away with his exotic refrains. Much of the attention paid to him as a 'popular' poet has been despicably motivated. It is to his credit that Antonio should have realized the small importance Manuel's *coplas* had in his work as a whole, in a remark reported by their brother José:[2] 'Manuel Machado es un inmenso poeta; pero para mí, el verdadero, el insuperable, no es como la generalidad de la gente cree: el de los cantares, sino el de todo lo demás.' If Manuel Machado has suffered as a superficial Andalusian, in the view of those who have never read or wish to ignore his best poetry, it is his own fault. He knew what he was doing. He shares the responsibility for the perversion of the originally generous faith of the Romantics in the idea of a 'popular' poet.

[1] 'Ahí quedan mis coplas, suspiros en el viento, gotas de agua en el mar de la poesía del pueblo...'
[2] *Últimas*, p. 41.

BIBLIOGRAPHY

I. WORKS BY MANUEL MACHADO

A. *The poems*

Over half a dozen editions of Machado's poetry claim to be complete. None of them is. But the loss is not grave because the poems usually omitted—the juvenile and the occasional poems—are those which can make the least claim on the attention of posterity. With few exceptions, a justified oblivion has overtaken the many poems that Machado did not rescue from reviews and minor collections in order to include them in the main 'complete' editions: those entitled *Obras completas, Poesía.* (*Opera omnia lyrica*), etc. But these 'complete' editions, while they have the advantage of being in this sense representative, have the great disadvantage of containing misprints, capricious variants and wrong datings, which, combined, obscure the pattern of Machado's development. A critical edition is still needed. For the purposes of this study further details of the poems are given where appropriate in a special index below.

Alma. Madrid, A. Marzo, [1902]. 138 pp. None of the copies I have seen bears a date. Machado himself said the book appeared 'a fines de 1900' (*Unos versos*, p. 75). Eight critics agree with him; six give 1901, twelve 1902. The position was further confused by M. García Blanco's incorrect dating of Unamuno's review of *Alma*, in his edition of Unamuno's essays *De esto y de aquello* (Buenos Aires, 1950), I, p. 184. The review is of March 1902, not 1901, and is a limit in one direction. And since later versions of the poems which appeared in *Electra* as late as May 1901 correspond more with *Alma* than with the original versions in *Electra*, it is unlikely that *Alma* preceded *Electra* or appeared much before the beginning of 1902.

Alma. (*Opera selecta*). Estudio crítico de Claudio Santos González. Paris, Garnier, (August) 1910. xvi and 280 pp. This second edition also includes poems from other books.

Alma. Museo. Los Cantares. Prólogo de Miguel de Unamuno. Madrid, Pueyo, 1907. xxvii and 160 pp. Many of the new poems in this collection first appeared in *Los Lunes del Imparcial* and *Renacimiento* (1906–7).

Antología. Madrid, Austral, 1940 (first of several editions). 153 pp.

Antología poética. Burgos, Ediciones Zugazaga, 1938.

Apolo. Teatro pictórico. Madrid, V. Prieto y Cía., (April) 1911. Most of these sonnets appeared during 1910 in *Blanco y Negro, La Ilustración española y americana* and *Los Lunes del Imparcial.*

Ars longa. Madrid, Ediciones Garcilaso, 1943. 456 pp. 'Reciente aún el éxito de *Cadencias de cadencias,* publica ahora este voluminoso *Ars longa*' (A. Moreno, *Escorial,* 38, December 1943, p. 231); I have not seen a copy of this work.

Ars moriendi. Madrid, Ed. Mundo latino, 1921. 100 pp. This book appeared either very late in 1921 or early in 1922, to judge from the dates of reviews and the fact that Machado had time to correct poems previously published in *Índice* (August–September 1921). Other poems previously in *Cosmopolis* and *La Libertad* (1919–20).

Cadencias de cadencias. Nuevas dedicatorias. Madrid, Editora Nacional, 1943. 207 pp. Some poems previously in *Escorial* (1942–3) and in the adolescent collection *Tristes y Alegres.*

Canciones y dedicatorias. Madrid, Imprenta hispano-alemana, 1915. 142 pp. Some poems previously in *Los Lunes del Imparcial, La Ilustración española y americana* and, naturally, in the volumes they introduced.

Cante hondo. Cantares, canciones y coplas, compuestas al estilo popular de Andalucía. Madrid, Imprenta Helénica, (January) 1912. 137 pp.

Cante hondo. Cantares, etc. Madrid, Renacimiento, (January) 1916. 139 pp. 2ª. edición, corregida y aumentada.

Cante hondo—Sevilla. San Sebastián, 1938. 177 pp. Ejemplar tirado expresamente para el autor.

Cante hondo—Sevilla. Seville, Aguilar, 1939. 150 pp. On pink paper.

Cante hondo—Sevilla. Madrid, Aguilar, s.d. 145 pp. Colección Brevarios.

Caprichos. Madrid, Tipografía de la Revista de Archivos, 1905. 157 pp. Some poems previously in *El Evangelio, Blanco y Negro* and *Helios* (1902–5).

Caprichos. Madrid, Imprenta Gutenberg, Castro y Cía., 1908. 157 pp. [2nd ed.]

El Mal Poema. Madrid, Imprenta Gutenberg, Castro y Cía., 1909. 155 pp.

Etcétera (con Enrique Paradas). Barcelona, López Robert, 1895. 126 pp. The only copy I have seen had one poem by Manuel Machado in it and this was on the last page. Since the copy was in bad condition and lacked an index, other poems by Machado may well have been lost.

Horario. Poemas religiosos. Madrid, Editora Nacional, 1947. 132 pp.

Horas de oro. Devocionario poético. Valladolid, Imprenta Castellana, 1938. 175 pp.

La fiesta nacional. Madrid, Fortanet, 1906. 15 pp.

Obras completas. Madrid, Ed. Mundo latino. In five volumes. I *Alma,* 1922. 198 pp. II *Museo. Apolo,* 1922. 142 pp. III *Cante hondo. Sevilla,* 1923. 182 pp. IV *El Mal Poema,* 1923. 182 pp. V (which includes much previously uncollected verse) *Dedicatorias,* 1924. 178 pp.

Obras completas. Madrid, Plenitud, 1947. 1338 pp. (including Antonio Machado). also 1951 (1249 pp.), 1954 (1400 pp.) and 1957 (1320 pp.).

Phoenix. Nuevas canciones. Madrid, Ediciones Héroe, 25 April 1936. 108 pp.

Poesía. (*Opera omnia lyrica*), Madrid, Editora Nacional, 1940. xix and 451 pp.

Poesía. (*Opera omnia lyrica*), Barcelona, Ediciones Jerarquía, 1940. xix and 451 pp.

Poesía. (*Opera omnia lyrica*), Madrid, Editora Nacional, 1942. 459 pp.

Poesías completas. Madrid, Residencia de Estudiantes, 1917.

Poesías escogidas. Prólogo de Miguel de Unamuno. Barcelona, Maucci, [1913]. 224 pp.

Poésias. (*Opera lyrica perfecta*). Madrid, Editora Internacional, s.d. 318 pp.

Poesías. (*Opera omnia lyrica*). Madrid, Editora Internacional, 1924. 318 pp.

Sevilla y otros poemas. Madrid, Editorial America, 1919. 138 pp.

Tristes y Alegres. Con Enrique Paradas. Contera de Salvador Rueda. Madrid, La Catalana, 1894. 111 unnumbered pages.

Trofeos. Barcelona, Gassó Hermanos, [1911]. 181 pp. It is in the list of *Obras publicadas* in the first edition of *Cante hondo*, below *Apolo*. It is a very carelessly produced volume containing many otherwise discarded poems from *Tristes y Alegres*.

Trofeos. Barcelona, Gassó Hermanos, 1920. 176 pp. (2nd edition.)

B. *Prose works*

Unlike Darío or Gómez Carrillo, Manuel Machado had no pretensions to being an important or revolutionary writer of prose. In fact in that medium he rarely produced more than a dozen consecutive pages. His published books of prose are without exception collections of short stories, critical essays, newspaper articles, prologues and speeches. Shortly before his marriage, it is true, he announced the forthcoming publication of two novels: *Lolita Valdés* and *De Montmartre al Barrio latino*. But neither ever appeared in print. If, as is probable, the latter eventually appeared as *El amor y la muerte*, the novel never became more than 'chapters of a novel'.

His output as a journalist was enormous; only a fraction of it is available in the collections listed below. Most, and much of the best, is still scattered in the newspapers and reviews mentioned below, and in others like: *A.B.C.*, *Cosmopolis*, *Diario de Huelva*, *El País*, *Escorial*, *Estafeta literaria*, *Juventud* (1946), *La caricatura*, *La Internacional*, *La Libertad*, *La Protesta*, *Le Journal*, *Los Lunes del Imparcial*, *Nuevo Mercurio*, *Revista de la Biblioteca*, *Archivo y Museo* and *Revista latina*.

Calderón y La vida es sueño (*Conferencia leída en el Teatro español para los niños de los asilos y escuelas municipales y provinciales*). Madrid, Imprenta municipal, 1918. 12 pp.

Día por día de mi calendario: memorandum de la vida española en 1918. Madrid, Pueyo, 1918. 179 pp. Weekly articles from *El Liberal*, January to June 1918.

Discurso pronunciado en el bicentenario de don Francisco de Goya y Lucientes, conmemorado por el Instituto de España en la Real Academia de Bellas Artes de San Fernando. Madrid, [1928].

El amor y la muerte. (*Capítulos de novela*). Madrid, Imprenta Helénica, 18 January 1913. 234 pp. Includes pieces from: *Alma española*, *Blanco y Negro*, *Helios*, *Juventud*, *Mundial Magazine* and *Revista ibérica*.

Estampas sevillanas. Madrid, A. Aguado, 1949. 159 pp. (Colección 'Más Allá' no.
    63). Many previously in *Arriba*; later all incorporated into *Obras completas*,
    Plenitud, 1951.
La Guerra Literaria. 1898–1914. (Crítica y ensayos). Madrid, Hispano-alemana,
    24 November 1913. 180 pp. Includes two speeches made for the Ministerio
    de Instrucción pública, 1911 and 1912, and pieces from *Helios, La Época*
    and *La Lectura.*
Un año de teatro. (Ensayos de crítica dramática). Madrid, Biblioteca nueva, [1917].
    208 pp. Reviews, twice and three times weekly, from *El Liberal*, 6 Novem-
    ber 1916 to 9 May 1917.
*Unos versos, un alma y una época. Discursos leídos en la Real Academia Española con
    motivo de la recepción de Manuel Machado.* (With J. M. Pemán). Madrid, Ed.
    Diana, 1940. 166 pp.

c. *The plays*

Manuel Machado wrote only one play single-handed, though he laid claim in
the fly-leaf of *La Guerra Literaria* to two others: *El poema del Cid* and *Villamediana*,
neither of which I have seen. His adaptations are listed in the next section with
his translations.

Amor al vuelo. (In one act and in collaboration with José Luis Montoto de Sedas).
    Seville, M. Hildago, 1904.
Desdichas de la fortuna o Julianillo Valcárcel. (In four acts and in collaboration
    with A. Machado). Madrid, F. Fé, 1926; Madrid, Imprenta Hispánica,
    1926; Madrid, Espasa Calpe, 1928; Madrid, Ed. C.I.A.P., 1932; Madrid,
    Ed. españolas, 1940; Barcelona, Cisne, 1942; Buenos Aires, Austral, 1951.
El hombre que murió en la guerra. (*Id.*). Buenos Aires, Austral, 1947.
El Pilar de la Victoria. (In two acts). Madrid, Editora Nacional, 1945.
Juan de Mañara. (In three acts and in collaboration with A. Machado). Madrid,
    Colección El Teatro, 1927; Madrid, Espasa Calpe, 1927; Madrid, Ed.
    C.I.A.P., 1932; Buenos Aires, Austral, 1942.
La duquesa de Benamejí. (*Id.*). Madrid, La farsa, 1932; Madrid, Ed. Dédalo, 1942;
    Buenos Aires, Austral, 1942.
La Lola se va a los puertos. (*Id.*). Madrid, La farsa, 1930—two editions; Madrid,
    Ed. C.I.A.P., 1932; Madrid, Ed. españolas, 1940; Madrid, Diana, 1944;
    Buenos Aires, Austral, 1951.
La prima Fernanda. (*Id.*). Madrid, La farsa, s.d.; Buenos Aires, Austral, 1942.
Las adelfas. (*Id.*). Madrid, La farsa, 1928; Madrid, Renacimiento, 1930; Madrid,
    Ed. C.I.A.P., 1932; Madrid, Ed. españolas, 1940; Buenos Aires, Austral,
    1947.

D. *Translations and adaptations*

Bayard, Émile. *El arte del buen gusto, estudio teórico y práctico de la belleza puesto
    al alcance de todos.* Paris, Garnier, 1909.
Bertrand, Louis. *Sanguis martyrum.* Paris, Garnier, 1921.

Beyle, Henri (Stendhal). *La Cartuja de Parma*. Paris, Garnier, 1909 (2 vols.).

Calderón de la Barca, Pedro. *El príncipe constante*. Madrid, La farsa, 1931.

Conan-Doyle, A. *El campamento de Napoleón*. Madrid, La novela ilustrada, s.d.

Crozière, Alphonse, *Lulú, novela alegre*. Paris, Garnier, 1909.

Daudet, Alphonse. *La novela de Caperuza-Roja*. Madrid, La novela ilustrada, s.d.

Descartes, René. *Obras completas*. Paris, Garnier, 1921 (2nd edition, 1938).

Hugo, Victor. *Hernani* (in collaboration with A. Machado and F. Villaespesa). Madrid, La farsa, 1928. First staged 1 January 1925.

La Rouchefoucauld. *Reflexiones, sentencias y máximas morales*. Paris, Garnier, 1914 (2nd edition, 1916).

Moréas, Jean. 'El rufián', *Electra*, 13 April 1901 (by 'Geminis'); also in *Cosmopolis*, March 1919, p. 563, under his own name.

Nordau, Max. *La batalla de los zánganos*. Madrid, La novela ilustrada, s.d.

Rostand, Edmond. *El aguilucho* (in collaboration with Luis de Oteyza). Madrid, La farsa, 1932. First staged 19 January 1920.

Sébillot, Paul. *Cuentos bretones, cuentos populares de campesinos, pescadores y marineros*. Paris, Garnier, 1900.

Spinoza, Baruch. *Ética*. Paris, Garnier, 1913.

Téllez, Gabriel. *El condenado por desconfiado* (in collaboration with A. Machado and José López). Madrid, La farsa, 1930. First staged 2 January 1924.

Van Leberghe, C. (untitled poems). *El Liberal*, 19 July 1918.

Vauvenargues. *Obras escogidas*. Paris, Garnier, 1914 (2nd edition, 1915).

Vega, Lope de. *El perro del hortelano* (in collaboration with A. Machado and José López). Madrid, La farsa, 1931. First staged 27 February 1931.

Hay verdades que en amor (in collaboration with A. Machado and José López). First staged in Salamanca, 1925.

La malcasada (in collaboration with J. M. Pemán and Amezúa). First staged 14 February 1947.

La niña de plata (in collaboration with A. Machado and José López). Madrid, La farsa, 1929. First staged 19 January 1926.

La viuda valenciana (in collaboration with A. Machado).

Verhaeren, Émile. 'Los pobres' and 'El molino', *El Liberal*, 4 July 1918.

Verlaine, Paul. *Fiestas galantes. Poemas saturnianos. La buena canción. Romanzas sin palabras. Sabiduría. Amor. Parábolas y otras poesías*. Prólogo de Enrique Gómez Carrillo. Madrid, Fortanet, 1908. 225 pp. (2nd edition, 1918).[1]

Virgil, *Obras*, Paris, Garnier, 1914.

---

[1] This literal prose translation was described by G. A. Tournoux, the author of a *Bibliographie Verlainienne*, as 'une des meilleures traductions qu'on ait faite en tout pays' (letter, Lille, March 1911, in the *BMB*).

II. WORKS ON MANUEL MACHADO

General literary and sociological surveys, and the usual manuals of criticism, are excluded except when they contain an account of Machado of unusual interest. Every scholarly work dealing directly with Machado is included, but a large number of newspaper articles treating him superficially has been omitted. By no means all the critical works mentioned in the book are listed.

Abril, Manuel. 'Caprichos', La Lectura, 5 (1905), 567–70.

'Bambalinas. Diablas y trastos', Buen Humor (Madrid), 4 November 1928.

Aguado, Emiliano. 'Cadencias de cadencias', Pueblo (Madrid), 23 December 1943.

Alberti, Rafael. 'Imagen sucesiva de Antonio Machado', Sur (Buenos Aires), 108 (1943), 7–16.

Albornoz, Aurora de. 'La caricatura', Ínsula, January–February 1962.

Aledo, Manuel G. de. 'Historia de dos versos de Don Manuel Machado', La Voz de España (San Sebastián), 28 January 1947.

Alfaro, José María. 'En la poética de Manuel Machado', Tajo (Madrid), 6 July 1940.

'Al borde de la poesía de Manuel Machado', Hoja de Lunes (Madrid), 20 January 1947.

Allué y Morer, Fernando. 'Un hermano de los Machado', Boletín de la Sociedad castellonense de Cultura (Castellón), XXXIV (1958), January–March, 66–9.

Almada, Luis. 'Los hermanos Machado. Poetas españoles', Estampa (Madrid), 6 September 1931.

Alonso, Dámaso. 'Ligereza y gravedad en la poesía de Manuel Machado', Revista de la biblioteca, archivo y museo, XVI (1947), 197–240; later in Poetas españoles contemporáneos, Madrid, Gredos, 1952, 50–102; latter edition used for quotations.

see Bousoño, Carlos.

Álvarez, Dictino. 'Cartas inéditas de Manuel Machado a Rubén Darío', Índice de Artes y Letras (Madrid), 118 (1958), 14. Subsequently published in Cartas de Rubén Darío, Madrid, Taurus, 1963.

Álvarez Fernández, P., 'Don Manuel Machado no va al cine. Ni quiere, ni puede', La estafeta literaria (Madrid), 8 (1944), 15.

Álvarez-Sierra, Dr J. 'Una tertulia matritense. ¿Quiénes son "los del 90"?', A.B.C., 18 November 1956.

'Enfermedad y muerte de Antonio Machado. Retorno a España', A.B.C., 21 February 1959.

Andrenio, see Gómez de Baquero, E.

Anon. 'Lo primero que escribieron nuestros grandes autores', Estampa (Madrid), 15 July 1933.

Armas Ayala, A. 'Epistolario de Manuel Machado', Índice de Artes y Letras, 50 (1952), 1 and 4.

Armiñán, Luis de. 'Manuel Machado ha muerto', *Diario de Barcelona*, 21 January 1947.

'Cuando Don Manuel fue Manolo', *A.B.C.*, 4 February 1947.

Arrarás, Joaquín. 'Fe y patriotismo de Manuel Machado', *Los Sitios* (Gerona), 9 February 1947.

Azorín, *see* Martínez Ruiz, J.

Balbontín, José Antonio. *Three Spanish Poets*, London, Alvin Redman, 1961. (Remarks on Manuel Machado in the section on his brother Antonio).

Baroja, Pío. *Desde la última vuelta del camino*, Madrid, Biblioteca nueva, 1945, III.

Bell, A. F. G. *Contemporary Spanish Literature*, London, Knopf, 1926.

Borrás, Tomás. '*Apolo*', *Libros y ideas* (Madrid), 1911.

'Manuel Machado académico', *Cuadernos de literatura contemporánea*, 2 (1942), 60.

Bousoño, Carlos. *Seis calas en la literatura española*, Madrid, Gredos, 1951, 235-9. (With D. Alonso.)

Teoría de la expresión poética, Madrid, Gredos, 1952, 75-6.

Brotherston, James Gordon. 'Manuel Machado y la pintura', *Boletín de la Institución Fernán-González* (Burgos), XLI (1962), no. 158, 117-19.

'Antonio Machado y Álvarez and Positivism', *Bulletin of Hispanic Studies* (Liverpool), XLI (1964), no. 4, 223-9.

Candamo, Bernardo G. de. 'Dos literaturas en una misma época', *El Liberal* (Madrid), 2 March 1917.

Cansinos Assens, Rafael (Cansino, Rafael). *La nueva literatura (1898. 1900. 1916)*, Madrid, Sanz Calleja, 1917, I, 185-92.

Los temas literarios y su interpretación, Madrid, Sanz Calleja, s.d., 112-40.

Cantu, Pablo. 'Manuel Machado ha dejado escritas sus memorias', *El Alcázar* (Madrid), 30 June 1948.

Carballo Picazo, Alfredo. '"Castilla" de Manuel Machado', in *Notas para un comentario de textos*, Páginas de la *Revista de Educación*, Madrid, 1963, 53-68.

Cardenal, M. 'Manuel Machado prosista', *Ínsula* (Madrid), 15 (March 1947).

Carrère, Emilio. 'Aquí Madrid', *Madrid*, 21 January 1947.

Cásseres, Marcella. 'El mundo poético de Manuel Machado', tesis doctoral leída en la Universidad de Madrid el 15 de junio de 1960.

Castellón, José. 'Lo que debe ser el teatro. Críticos y empresarios. Manuel Machado', *La Tribuna*, 12 September 1919.

Cejador y Frauca, Julio. *Historia de la lengua y literatura castellana*, Madrid, Revista del Archivo, Biblioteca y Museo, 1920, XII, 59-61.

Cerdan Gómez, José, 'Manuel Machado en el olvido. (Estética)', *La Correspondencia de Valencia*, 15 July 1936.

Chabás y Martí, Juan. 'Manuel Machado: Poesías. Opera omnia lyrica', *Revista de Occidente* 6 (1924), 286-96.

'Crítica concéntrica de Manuel Machado', *Alfar* (Corunna), April 1925, 4-10.

Breve historia de la literatura española, Barcelona, J. Gil, 1933. (2nd edition, 1936.)

'Manuel Machado', in *Vuelo y estilo. Estudios de literatura contemporánea*, Madrid, Sociedad general española de librería, 1934, I, 97–125.

Nueva y manual historia de la literatura española, La Habana, Cultural, 1953.

Chispero. 'El talento no envejece', *Informaciones* (Madrid), 19 August 1940.

Cossío, José María de. *Los toros en la poesía castellana*, Madrid, C.I.A.P., 1931, I, 295–305 and II, 337–45.

'Recuerdo de Manuel Machado', *Arriba*, 13 February 1947.

Cincuenta años de poesía española (1850–1900), Madrid, Espasa Calpe, 1960, I, 614–20.

Cossío, Manuel B. 'Homenaje a los poetas Manuel y Antonio Machado', in *Desdichas de la fortuna*, Madrid, Imp. Hispánica, 1926.

Darío, Rubén. 'La fiesta nacional', in *Prosa dispersa, Obras completas*, Madrid, Mundo latino, 1919, XX, 43–55.

'Nuevos poetas de España', in *Opiniones*, Madrid, Mundo latino, 1920, X, 189–96.

D'Artedo, Ivan. 'La jacarandosa poesía de Manuel Machado', *Misión* (Madrid), 15 February 1947.

Del Hoyo Torrens, A. 'Manuel Machado', *El Pirineo* (Gerona), 7 November 1942.

Díaz-Plaja, Guillermo. *Modernismo frente a 98*, Madrid, Espasa Calpe, 1951.

Diego, Gerardo. *Poesía española. Antología 1912–1931*, Madrid, Editoral Signo, 1932 (2nd edition, 1934). First edition used for quotations.

'Machado el mayor', *A.B.C.*, 26 January 1947.

'Los dos Manueles', *Solidaridad Nacional* (Barcelona), 30 January 1947.

'Manuel Machado (1874–1947)', *Revista de Indias* (Madrid), VIII (1948), 33–4 (July–December), 1165–1172.

'Poetas de la generación del 98', *Arbor* (Madrid), 36 (December 1948), 439–48.

Diego, Juan de. 'La última observación de Manuel Machado', *Levante* (Valencia), 31 January 1947.

Díez-Canedo, Enrique. '*Poesías escogidas*', *Revista de Libros* (Madrid), August 1913, 5–6.

'Los dos hermanos poetas', *La Nación* (Buenos Aires), 3 June 1923.

Reviews of the Machados' plays in the following numbers of *Sol*: 18 May 1926, 18 March 1927, 23 October 1928, 9 November 1929 and 27 March 1932.

Díez Herrero, Diego. 'Huelva en la biografía de Manuel Machado', *Diario de Huelva*, 1947.

Doreste Silva, Luis. 'Los poetas se van', *Falange* (Las Palmas), 22 January 1947.

D'Ors, Eugenio: see Ors, Eugenio d'.

Dumont, Maurice. 'Antonio et Manuel Machado', 'Lettres espagnoles', *Cassandre* (Brussels), 22 June 1935.

F.B., D. 'Don Manuel Machado', *Santo y Seña* (Madrid), 30 July 1942.

Fernández Almagro, Melchor, 'La poésie et la guerre', *Occident* (Paris), 1 (March 1940), 86–9.

'"Poesía" por Manuel Machado', *A.B.C.*, 16 June 1940.

Manuel Machado: los primeros versos', *A.B.C.*, 22 January 1947; later collected with 'A cabo de los años' in *En torno al 98. Política y Literatura*, Madrid, Jordan, 1948, 165–70 and 170–2 respectively.

'Otro poeta y un actor', *Vanguardia* (Barcelona), 5 February 1947.

'Juan Ramón Jiménez y algunos poetas andaluces de su juventud', *Homenaje a Dámaso Alonso*, Madrid, Gredos, 1960, I, 493–507.

Ferreres, Rafael. 'Manuel Machado', *Cuadernos de literatura contemporánea*, 2 (1942), 61–2.

Figueroa d'Oliveira, José. 'Manuel Machado, poeta de Espanha', *O comercio do Porto* (Oporto), 25 January 1947.

Gallardo, Francisco. 'El poeta Manuel Machado y su vida en Burgos', *El Diario de Ávila*, 26 July 1947.

García Vino, M. 'Una poesía indudablemente andaluza: la flamenca', *Estafeta literaria*, 15 February 1962.

Ghiraldo, Alberto. *El archivo de Rubén Darío*, Buenos Aires, Losada, 1943, 429–30.

Giralda Adams, Lula, *Rimas y versos*, New York, Century, 1929. (With Ruth Lansing).

Gómez de Baquero, Eduardo. 'Crónica literaria', *La España moderna*, 226 (October 1907).

'Apolo', *Los Lunes del Imparcial*, 10 April 1911.

'Nuevos versos de Manuel Machado', *La Época* (Madrid), 6 May 1922. Later collected as 'El Ars moriendi de Manuel Machado' in *Pen Club I: Los poetas*, Madrid, Renacimiento, 1929, 229–33.

Gómez Carrillo, Enrique. 'El sexto sentido', *La Razón* (Buenos Aires), 30 July (1918?).

Prologue to *Fiestas galantes* (1908).

Gómez de la Serna, Ramón. 'Manuel Machado', in *Nuevos retratos contemporáneos*, Buenos Aires, Editorial sudamericana, 1945, 29–39.

Automoribundia (1888–1948), Buenos Aires, ibid., 1948.

González Blanco, Andrés. 'Manuel Machado', *Nuestro tiempo*, VI (1906), 3, 72–178; later collected in *Los contemporáneos. Apuntes para una historia de la literatura hispano-americana a principios del siglo xx*, Paris, Garnier, 1909, II, 83–124.

González-Climent, Anselmo. *Antología de poesía flamenca*, Madrid, Escelicer, 1961, 31–56 and 242–7.

González-Ruano, César. *Antología de poetas españoles contemporáneos*, Barcelona, Gustavo Gili, 1946, 83–91.

'Esa música vaga', *Arriba*, 29 January 1947.

Las palabras quedan, Madrid, A. Aguado, 1957.

González Ruiz, Nicolás. 'Manuel Machado y el lirismo polifónico', *Cuadernos de literatura contemporánea*, 2 (1942), 63–78.

'Manuel Machado. El poeta andaluz', *Ideal* (Granada), 1 February 1947.

Granjel, Luis. *Panorama de la generación del 98*, Madrid, Guadarrama, 1959.

Guerra, Manuel Henry. *El teatro de Manuel y Antonio Machado*, Madrid, Editorial Mediterráneo, 1966.

Guerrero Ruiz, Juan. *Juan Ramón, de viva voz*, Madrid, Ínsula, 1961.

Guillén, Jorge. 'La retirada de Manuel Machado. Circunloquios', *La Libertad*, 28 March 1922.

Gullón, Ricardo. *Conversaciones con Juan Ramón Jiménez*, Madrid, Taurus, 1958.

'Relaciones amistosas y literarias entre Antonio Machado y Juan Ramón Jiménez', *La Torre* (Puerto Rico), 25 (January 1959), 159–215.

'Relaciones literarias entre Juan Ramón y Villaespesa', *Ínsula* (Madrid), 149 (April 1959), 1–2.

'Relaciones amistosas y literarias entre Juan Ramón Jiménez y Manuel Machado', *Cuadernos hispano-americanos* (Madrid), 127 (July 1960), 115–39.

Relaciones amistosas y literarias entre Juan Ramón Jiménez y los Martínez Sierra, Puerto Rico, La Torre, 1961.

Direcciones del Modernismo, Madrid, Gredos, 1963.

Henríquez Ureña, Max. *Breve historia del Modernismo*, Mexico, Fondo de Cultura Económica, 1954.

Iruña, Fermín de. 'La amable erudición de Manuel Machado', *El Alcázar* (Madrid), 21 January 1947.

Jiménez, Juan Ramón. 'Alma y capricho de Manuel Machado', *La corriente infinita*, Madrid, Aguilar, 1961, 41–6; quotations have also been made from other articles in this collection.

El Modernismo. Notas de un curso (1923), Mexico, Aguilar, 1962.

see Gullón, Ricardo.

Jiménez, Manuel. 'Rincón Lazcano habla de los 30 años que lleva Manuel Machado en el Ayuntamiento', *Arriba*, 11 September 1944.

Juretschke, Hans. *Das Frankreichbild des modernen Spanien*, Bonn, Poppinghaus, 1937, 84–5.

Kendall, J. S. '*Ars moriendi*, by Manuel Machado', *Double Dealer* (London), February 1923, 85.

Laborde, Jules. 'Vie littéraire. Le mouvement littéraire en Espagne', *La vie des peuples* (Paris-Bourdeaux), 52 (August 1924), 829–31.

Laín Entralgo, Pedro. 'Manuel Machado y el noventa y ocho', *A.B.C.*, 27 December 1945 (part I) and *A.B.C.*, 28 December 1945 (part II).

'Recuerdo de Manuel Machado', *A.B.C.*, 24 December 1947. These two articles were collected under the title 'En torno a Manuel Machado' in *Vestigios*, Madrid, E.P.E.S.A., 1948, 117–25.

Lansing, Ruth, *see* Giralda Adams, Lula.

Las Navas, Eliseo de. 'Manuel Machado ha cumplido 70 años', *Fotos* (Madrid), 393 (9 September 1944).

Lázaro, Ángel. 'Lectura de Antonio y Manuel Machado', *Semblanzas y ensayos*, Puerto Rico, Universidad de Puerto Rico, 1963, 223–8.

Lázaro Carreter, Fernando. 'La poesía de Manuel Machado', a talk given on *Radio Zaragoza*, 29 January 1943.

Lepiorz, Gerhard. *Themen und Ausdrucksformen des spanischen Symbolismus*, Düsseldorf, G. H. Nolte, 1938.

'Manuel Machado (1874–1947)', *Romanische Forschungen* (Frankfurt), 61 (1948), 388–92.

Ley, Charles David, 'Homenaje', *El Español* (Madrid), 25 January 1947.

Spanish poetry since 1939, Washington, Catholic University of America Press, 1962, 20–1.

Linares, Manuel. 'Manuel Machado habla de su espíritu. Notas a un capítulo inédito de su vida', *Razón y Fe* (Madrid), 611 (1948), 647–62.

López Lapuya, Isidoro. *La Bohemia española en París a fines del siglo pasado*, Paris, Ibero-americano, 1927.

López Ruiz, J. 'Entierro de los restos mortales del ilustre poeta Manuel Machado', *Falange* (Las Palmas), 21 January 1947.

López Sancho, J. 'Manuel Machado, puente de la poesía española', *Ideal Gallego* (Corunna), 21 January 1947.

López-Tresastro, Cayetano. 'Manuel Machado. El "ángel" de su poesía', *El Español* (Madrid), 18 March 1944.

Lujan, Nestor. 'La muerte de Manuel Machado', *Destino* (Barcelona), 25 January 1947.

Machado y Ruiz, Joaquín. 'Relámpagos del recuerdo', *Atenea* (Santiago de Chile), xxviii (1951), 312 (June), 377–84.

Machado y Ruiz, José. *Últimas soledades del poeta Antonio Machado*, typewritten, Santiago de Chile (1948).

Macrí, Oreste. *Poesia spagnola del novacento*, Parma, Guanda, 1952.

Antonio Machado, Milan, Lerici, 1962, 21.

McVan, Alice Jane. *Antonio Machado*, New York, Hispanic Society of America, 1959, 5–7.

Maffiotte, Ildefonso. 'Hombres y cosas de Madrid. Manuel Machado', *La Prensa* (Madrid), 22 August 1933.

Mantero, Manuel. 'Los toros en la poesía', *Ínsula* (Madrid), 176–7 (1960), 8.

Martínez Ruiz, José. 'Antonio y Manuel', *A.B.C.*, 13 April 1947.

Martínez Sierra, Gregorio. *Renacimiento* (Madrid), 3 (May 1907).

Marx, Olga. 'Felipe IV', *Poet Lore*, 30 (1919), 615–16.

Miranda, Ledesma. 'El "ángel" de Manuel Machado. Presencias y mensajes', *Arriba*, 18 May 1944.

Montesinos, J. F. *Die moderne spanische Dichtung*, Leipzig–Berlin, Teubner, 1927.

Montoto y Rautenstrauch, Luis. *Por aquellas calendas*, Madrid, Renacimiento, 1930, 104–7.

Moreno, Alfonso. 'Ars longa por Manuel Machado', *Escorial*, 37–8 (November–December 1943), 231.

Poesía española actual, Madrid, Ed. Nacional, 1946, 31–46.

Moreno Villa, José. *Vida en claro (autobiografía)*, Mexico, El Colegio de México, 1944.

'Manuel Machado, la Manolería y el cambio', *Los autores como actores*, Mexico, *ibid.*, 1951.

Moya, M. J. 'Preguntas de *El Alcázar*', *El Alcázar*, 14 April 1943.

Narbona, Rafael. 'El gran poeta Manuel Machado. Lo que eran los autores a los veinte años', *La Voz* (Madrid), 9 October 1933.

'Horario por Manuel Machado', *Emisión Radio España*, 12 March 1947.

Nervo, Amado. 'Manuel Machado', *Obras completas*, Madrid, Aguilar, 1956, II, 388.

Núñez, Antonio. 'En torno a las figuras del 98' (an interview with R. Calvo), *Ínsula*, 236–7 (July–August 1966).

Obregón, Antonio de. 'Estreno de...*El hombre que murió en la guerra*', *Arriba*, 19 April 1941.

Oliver Belmás, Antonio. *Este otro Rubén Darío*, Barcelona, Aedos, 1960.

Onís, Federico de. *Antología de la poesía española e hispano-americana*, Madrid, Centro de Estudios históricos, 1934.

Orozco Díaz, E. 'Poesía juvenil y juventud poética en la obra de Manuel Machado', *Nuestro Tiempo* (Madrid), 16 (October 1955), 17–29.

Ors, Eugenio d', 'Novísimo glosario. ¿ Ars moriendi?', *Arriba*, 23 January 1947.

Ortega y Gasset, Eduardo. 'Al margen del libro', *Los Lunes del Imparcial*, 22 July 1912.

'Manuel Machado. Letras españolas', *El Universal Ilustrado*, 24 March 1927.

Ortiz, R. *Poeti spagnoli di ieri e di oggi*, iii, Rome, 1941.

Ortiz de Pinedo, José. 'La poesía en Manuel Machado', *El Alcázar* (Madrid), 12 August 1940.

Pamplona, Fernando de. 'Ineditismo e originalidade', *Diario de Manhá* (Lisbon), 24 April 1945.

Paradas, Enrique. 'Manuel Machado', *Diario de Cádiz*, 24 December 1922.

Peers, E. Allison. *Cuarenta sonetos españoles*, Liverpool, Bulletin of Spanish Studies, 1933.

A History of the Romantic Movement in Spain, Cambridge, 1940. 2 vols.

'Two poems by Manuel Machado. New interpretations of Spanish poetry', *Bulletin of Spanish Studies* (Liverpool), 18 (1941), 229–30.

Pellicer Cámara, Carlos. *Poemas de Antonio y Manuel Machado. Selección e impresiones*, Mexico, Cultura, 1917.

Pemán, José María. *La poesía de Manuel Machado como documento humano*, Madrid, Diana, 1940. (Bound with *Unos versos*.)

'Don Manuel Machado', *Boletín de la Real Academia Española*, xxvi (1947), 7–17.

Pérez Ferrero, Miguel. 'La última tertulia literaria de los Machado', *A.B.C.*, 19 May 1946.

'En la hora de la muerte de Manuel Machado', *Patria* (Granada), 22 January 1947.

'Paradas y "La Caricatura"', *Arriba* (Madrid), 19 February 1947.

'El París de Manuel Machado', *Ínsula* (Madrid), 15 (15 March 1947).

Vida de Antonio Machado y Manuel, Buenos Aires, Austral, 1952.

Pérez Zalabardo, María de la Concepción. 'Sobre la muerte y la vida de Antonio Machado', *Revista de Literatura*, xv, 104–11.

Puccini, Mario. 'Letteratura spagnola. Fombona–Machado–Chabás', *Giornale di Letteratura e di Politica*, December 1927, 2–3.

Répide, Pedro de. 'Lira y guitarra', *Domingo* (Madrid), January 1947.

Ribbans, Geoffrey W. 'La influencia de Verlaine en Antonio Machado', *Cuadernos Hispano-Americanos* (Madrid), 91–2 (1957), 180–201.

Riqueza inagotada de las revistas literarias modernistas, Madrid, Revista de Literatura, 1958.

'Unamuno and Antonio Machado', *Bulletin of Hispanic Studies* (Liverpool), 34, 10–38.

'Unamuno and the younger writers in 1904', *ibid.* 35, 83–100.

Rodríguez Alcalde, Leopoldo. 'Elegía y reivindicación de don Manuel Machado', *Alerta* (Santander), 22 January 1947.

Romo Arregui, J. 'Manuel Machado. Bibliografía', *Cuadernos de literatura contemporánea*, 2 (1942), 79–81.

Rueda, Salvador. 'Contera' in *Tristes y Alegres*.

Ruiz Cabriada, Agustín. *Bio-bibliografía del Cuerpo facultativo de Archiveros, Bibliotecarios y Arqueólogos*, Madrid, 1958.

Sampelayo, Juan. 'Una hora con Manuel Machado. Charlas literarias', *Arriba* (Madrid), 28 September 1941.

'Manuel Machado en su jubilación', *A.B.C.*, 30 August 1944.

Santos González, C. Prologue to *Alma*, 2nd edition (1911).

Sassone, Felipe. *La rueda de mi fortuna*, Madrid, Aguilar, 1958.

Sawa, Alejandro. 'Ante un libro', *Los Lunes del Imparcial*, 23 March 1908.

Servicio de extensión cultural y artística de la delegación local de Juventudes. 'La poesía de Manuel Machado', *Radio Tarrasa*, June 1962.

Souvirón, José María. 'Personas. Manuel Machado', *A.B.C.*, 8 June 1962.

Trend, J. B. 'The brothers Machado', *Times Literary Supplement*, 20 May 1926. Later in *Alfonso the Sage*, London, St John's Minority Press, 1926, 135–46.

Unamuno, Miguel de. 'El Alma de Manuel Machado', *Heraldo de Madrid*, 19 March 1902; later in *De esto y de aquello*, Buenos Aires, Editoral sud-americana, 1950, I, 184–92.

Prologue to *Alma. Museo. Los Cantares*, dated 'Salamanca, IV, 07'; reprinted as a prologue to *Poesías escogidas*, with slight revisions.

'Otro arabesco pedagógio', *Los Lunes del Imparcial*, 22 December 1913; later in *Inquietudes y meditaciones*, Madrid, A. Aguado, 1957, 123–9.

'Manuel Machado y yo. Arabesco tópico literario', *Los Lunes del Imparcial*, 5 January 1914; later in *Mi vida y otros recuerdos personales*, Buenos Aires, Losada, 1959, I, 134–8.

Urbina, Luis G. 'Guía de un soñador', *El Universal* (Mexico), 22 December 1929.

Vian, Francesco. *Il modernismo nella poesia ispanica*, Milan, La Goliardica, 1955, 230–41.

Viu, Francisco de. 'Manuel y Antonio Machado disertan como convencidos republicanos', *Ahora* (Madrid), April 1931.

Vivanco, Luis Felipe. 'El poeta de "Adelfos"', *Escorial* (Madrid), 6 (April 1941), 140–8.

'La muerte de Manuel Machado', *Correo Literario*, II (1951), 16.

Warren, L. A. *Modern Spanish Literature*, London, Brentano, 1929, II, 453–60.

Zugazaga, José María. 'Retrato de Manuel Machado', typewritten, 31 June 1941.

'Conversación con Manuel Machado', *Solidaridad Nacional* (Barcelona), 17 December 1943.

'Manuel Machado presintió su muerte', *Pueblo* (Madrid), 20 January 1947.

'In memoriam Manuel Machado', *Diario de Burgos*, 29 January 1947.

INDEXES

NAMES